Saying Good-Bye

**A Manager's Guide
to Employee Dismissal**

Saying Good-Bye

A Manager's Guide to Employee Dismissal

Paula Michal-Johnson
Lehigh University

Scott, Foresman and Company
Glenview, Illinois • London, England

Acknowledgments

The excerpts on page 14 (Figure 1.4), from Patricia King's 1984 book, *Performance Planning and Appraisal,* are quoted with permission from McGraw-Hill Book Company.

The case studies on pages 60–63 are reprinted with permission from James Schreier, Marquette University, College of Business Administration, Milwaukee, WI. Several of the cases were also published in an article, "Training for Terminations," published in December, 1980. Copyright 1980, *Training and Development Journal,* American Society for Training and Development. Reprinted with Permission. All rights reserved.

The model on page 73 from "The Terminated Executive: It's Like Dying," by M. Finley and T. Lee, is reprinted with permission of *The Personnel and Guidance Journal.*

The models in Figures 5-1 and 5-3 are taken from Mark Knapp's book *Social Intercourse: From Greeting to Good-bye.* Permission to reprint is granted from Allyn & Bacon and Co. © 1978.

Figure 6.1 is reprinted, by permission, from Lawrence B. Rosenfeld, *Now That We're All Here: Relations in Small Groups.* Copyright 1976 by Charles E. Merrill.

Figure 6.3 is reprinted with permission from Jack R. Gibb, *The Journal of Communication,* and the International Communication Association for "Defensive Communication," which appeared in Volume 11, No. 3 (1961).

Library of Congress Cataloging in Publication Data

Michal-Johnson, Paula.
  Saying good-bye.

  Bibliography
  Includes index.
  1. Employees, Dismissal of.   I. Title.
HF5549.5.D55M53   1985   658.3'13   85-2194
ISBN 0-673-15843-8

ISBN 0-673-15843-8

1 2 3 4 5 6 7 - KPF - 90 89 88 87 86 85

CONTENTS

3

COMMUNICATING THE DIFFICULT MESSAGE OF TERMINATION   35

4

AFTER THE INTERVIEW: WHAT NOW?   67

5

DEVELOPING STRATEGIES TO DETECT TROUBLED RELATIONSHIPS   83

6

WHAT MAKES IT SO HARD?   96

PREFACE

As the title suggests, this book is intended to assist managers who must understand, prepare for, and implement dismissals. It is not a legal reference book or a personnel procedures manual; instead, it is designed to address those key problems that make communicating the message of dismissal so difficult. Handling interviews in an effective and equitable way is often a matter of how we say "good-bye."

While many human resource administrators are aware of this truth, it is often hard to ensure that as managers, we are trained to cope with dismissals. Even when training is attempted, it may be difficult to use in practice. Several years ago the personnel director of my organization asked me to develop a training unit for our managers on conducting dismissals. When all the plans for the seminar were completed, he apologetically called to say, "I'm afraid we will have to cancel the seminars. Word has gotten out that our managers are taking a crash course in firing and many of our employees are afraid there will be a purge." Dismissal, or even the rumor of it, can strike fear into the heart of the workforce.

Dismissal is the unspoken paranoia of the marketplace. In fact, the examples used in this book have been altered to protect the anonymity of the companies and managers. All company names have been changed, as have individual managers' names, to protect them from reprisals. Without the promise of confidentiality, it is doubtful that this guide could have been written. For whatever reasons, discussion of termination practices sends up a red flag for many organizations.

With the promise of complete confidentiality, scores of people who have been caught in the Catch-22 of the firing line agreed to talk to me. Their stories are gripping and often filled with regret. Among their reactions there is a common thread. Everyone, regardless of which side of the desk they sit on, wishes there was a better way to communicate the message of dismissal. By and large, managers would rather take a time-release capsule that allowed them to handle the process painlessly. Unfortunately, there are no drugs that will make it easier. Employees, with a slightly different perspective, want dismissals to be handled with respect and concern.

While this book does not pretend to be all things for all people, it can be read in several different ways. If, as a manager, you want immediate guidance for an impending dismissal, you may want to concentrate on certain chapters. Since the first chapter establishes the need for conducting more effective dismissals and clarifies the relationship between terminations and other vital employment processes, it is possible to read it later. Likewise, Chapters Five and Six explain the rationale behind the specific suggestions for conducting dismissals. So, if you are most interested in finding help quickly, you may want to read Chapters Two, Three, and Four first. The brief synopses of these chapters may allow you to even further streamline your reading efforts.

If, on the other hand, you are free to take a more leisurely approach to your reading, and are interested in a more theoretical understanding of the problem, you will find Chapters One, Five, and Six most helpful. In fact, if you are operating from this second mental framework I would suggest reading the book in the following order: Chapter One, Chapter Two, Chapter Five, Chapter Six, Chapter Three, and Chapter Four.

Chapter One—Why Care?

The reasons for caring about how we conduct dismissals are spelled out in the first chapter. The specific financial, legal, and personal costs that inevitably accompany discharges are cited. In fact, such reasons clarify the need for training in the conduct of dismissals. The second half of the chapter explains that firings are not isolated events. Dismissals are often necessitated by errors made in selection interviews and performance appraisals. A model of the employment cycle illustrates the dynamic connections between the actions taken by employers and the corresponding actions of employees and vice versa.

Chapter Two—The Dismissal Interview: Issues to Consider

The interview for dismissal is discussed in this chapter as a primary managerial responsibility. Incorporated into this chapter are the key causes of dismissal, the importance of the organization's philosophy of dismissal, the role of arbitrators, and a checklist for managing dismissals. You may find the checklist and the personal inventory for managers to be a helpful place to begin your study of dismissals if your time is limited.

Chapter Three—Communicating the Difficult Message of Termination

Professional football coaches tell us that training is a crucial element in the success of their football teams. In this spirit, Chapter Three offers suggestions for developing an effective game plan for the terminations we will conduct. It specifies ways to organize the interview and convey the message, based on the reason for termination and the nature of our relationship with the employee.

Chapter Four—After the Interview: What Now?

Just as good coaches review the game films with their players to correct decision errors and performance problems, managers can evaluate their own successes or failures in the dismissal interview. Chapter Four suggests a strategy for placing the dismissal in perspective and learning from it. The plight of the employee and the options available to him or her are also detailed here.

Chapter Five—Developing Strategies to Detect Troubled Relationships

Based on the work of Irving Altman, Donald Taylor, and Mark Knapp, this chapter establishes a model that helps explain the evolution of supervisory-subordinate relationships from first through final encounters. The model assumes there are ten possible stages that can reflect the specific nature of each relationship. In conjunction with this model, a diagnostic process is presented that allows managers to examine the quality of their own relationships with subordinates based on a series of communication strategies. The diagnostic tools offer us opportunities to perform preventive maintenance on our work relationships.

Chapter Six—What Makes It So Hard?

Gerald Jampolsky's work with terminally ill children and their fearful attitudes—described in his book, *Love Is Letting Go of Fear*—serves as a cornerstone for understanding the factors that promote fear in conducting dismissals. This chapter examines how fear inhibits us from coping effectively with interpersonal conflict, defensive communication, and change. When we understand that our attitudes toward each of these factors directly affects the outcome of the dismissal interviews we conduct, we are in a better position to manage the fear and thus the interview.

Appendix—Case Studies

The cases in this section are based on incidents reported to the author. They can be used as test cases to help us assess our own reactions to the validity of the dismissal and the actions taken in the interview. The cases may be used in conjunction with the training module in Chapter Three to help prepare managers for dismissals.

All in all, this book offers support to those of us who are called upon to dismiss employees. If we can translate the observations and suggestions in this guide into productive action, then the book has succeeded. If we are able to use the methods in the book, then managers and their departing employees will have benefitted from this guide.

We can think of the guide as a map of the territory of dismissal. We all know that it is safer to leave for a trip with a roadmap in hand than to strike out with no real sense of direction. Maps inform us of our travel options and the dangers of particular routes. In much the same way, this book examines the options that are available to us as we consider the dismissal of employees.

No book is a solo production and this one is no exception. Many people took part in this effort. In the conceptualization of the book, Lyman W. Porter and Joseph W. McGuire offered clear and substantive guidance that has made the book clearer. Sara Alpern of Texas A&M University has contributed selflessly to page-by-page revisions of all drafts of this enterprise, improving its readability. Also, Ron Zemke of *Training* provided a review of the book that has, hopefully, made it more useful for practitioners. Ron Bossert of Mack Trucks, Inc., also critiqued the first four chapters to ensure that my academic training did not obscure what I was really trying to say.

The impetus for this book, however, was the encouragement of graduate professors at the University of Denver. Alvin Goldberg, Carl Larson, Alton Barbour, and Donna Jurick supported my research of termination interviews. Mark Knapp's discussion of his book *Social Intercourse: From Greeting to Goodbye* in a 1978 seminar at the University of Denver actually spawned this study of employee dismissal. Other supporters who figure prominently in the cheering section for this book include Roger Holloway of Scott, Foresman and Company and both Helmut Esau and Elisabeth Hardy. David Johnson, the long-suffering spouse who has lived through writing and revisions to the point of nausea, also deserves to celebrate this finished work.

PAULA MICHAL-JOHNSON

Saying Good-Bye

**A Manager's Guide
to Employee Dismissal**

1

WHY CARE?

As Bob Townsend, vice-president of AGR, sat at his desk one morning, he tried to calm down. It was 9:15 and he had already downed his second cup of office coffee, but the coffee didn't ease the knot in his stomach. He was anxious about the meeting he had set up with Jerry Reynolds, his office manager of five years. Bob knew that Jerry could not work for AGR any longer. The stack of complaints from office employees and customers was convincing enough. Nonetheless, he was still reluctant to fire Jerry. Jerry had been with the company since its beginning but had refused to make changes that would make the office more effective. Bob thought he had made it clear to Jerry that things really had to change. Jerry had not taken him seriously. He didn't know why. Maybe it was because Bob and Jerry were in the same poker group and Jerry just did not believe that Bob would take action. "Well," Bob gulped, "there's no time like the present." As Jerry walked into Bob's office, Bob found himself saying, "Jerry, please sit down; we have to talk very seriously about your job here."

The Nature of Dismissals

With different names and circumstances, this scene is repeated daily in companies throughout the United States. Whether we choose to call it dismissal, separation, dehiring, termination, discharge, or firing, the end result is the same. A person loses a job, a company loses an employee, and a nation gains an unemployment statistic. There are no clear indications of how many people are dismissed every year. State and federal agencies that keep unemployment statistics lump employees who are fired in the same category with those who die or become disabled. The figures are further muddied because we cannot know how many resignations are really disguised dismissals. Virtually anyone may be fired, regardless of his or her length of service to a company or position. Line operators, supervisors, and those on up the executive ladder are all subject to dismissal. It was estimated that upwards of 20,000 executives were fired in 1981 alone.

A Definition of Dismissal

For our purposes in this book, all involuntary dismissals, whether for cause or economic necessity, will be considered. Involuntary dismissals all have several things in common. First, they are initiated by the manager of the employee (or someone on up the line). Second, ideally they are caused by a *legitimate* need. Third, and perhaps the most obvious, they signal a major disruption in the relationship between the company and the employee and between the employee and his or her job-related identity. Dismissals are one of the most delicate of all managerial responsibilities. So before we go any further, we need to ask ourselves, "Why care about the handling of dismissals?"

Reasons for Caring About Dismissals

Because of the financial and personal costs involved, we owe it to ourselves to carefully consider how we proceed in terminations. The financial costs may include replacement of the terminee (with the predictable expenses of advertising, recruiting, interviewing, and screening) as well as potential nuisance costs associated with extensive lawsuits and/ or revenge actions such as theft of property or damage to valuable company resources. Though these costs are significant, they are easier to calculate than the other personal costs of dismissal, which represent a comparable loss on the human investment. Those employees who work with or for the employee to be dismissed are inevitably affected. The morale of the workforce often suffers from the loss. The psychological pressures and stress of dismissal can also affect the manager's productivity and effectiveness. Let us explore each of these costs in greater depth.

Financial Costs

Turnover Costs It is surprising to discover how much organizations pay to replace someone who has been dismissed. If the dismissed employee is a secretary, the replacement cost ranges between $10,000 and $18,000. Sound exorbitant? It's not. Mobley (1982) tells us that employee turnover is a costly aspect of American manufacturing and business. The costs to consider when you are thinking of firing someone include: (1) the amount of time you must endure being without the services of the person; (2) the number of hours you must work in addition to your normal workload; (3) the investment in fees to employment agencies for recruiting, interviewing, and training; (4) unemployment insurance contributions to the dismissed employee; (5) the severance package of salary and benefits afforded the terminee; and (6) the length of time it takes the new employee to learn the system so he or she functions at least as well as the dismissed employee.

We have an investment in every employee we hire and fire. Mirvis and Lawler (1977) estimated that it costs more than $2,500 when a bank teller quits. The turnover costs for a moderately successful Texas oil company are staggering:

Secretary $18,000
Rig hand $5,000
Manager $73,000

Independent of these costs, the same company spent $380,000 in one year for the services of employment agencies, executive recruiters and outplacement services. These figures underscore why managers must think twice before terminating an employee.

Few organizations have systematically assigned monetary value to all of their positions so that they can determine turnover losses on their investments in employees, but those who have are always amazed at the financial drain that occurs through resignations and dismissals. If turnover costs are a concern for you, Mobley's book *Employee Turnover: Causes, Consequences and Control* (1982) may be of value.

Legal Costs   The responsibility of implementing fair employment practices rests with the employer. Careful, not capricious, evaluation and review of each case of dismissal assists in reducing the potential for litigation. One Denver lawsuit that warranted a generous out-of-court settlement for $500,000 dollars lasted two years and consumed the time and effort of the managerial staff for the same period of time. Had they reviewed the legal aspects of the case, their decision to terminate would have been withdrawn.

There is little doubt that we live in a society that views the legal system as the appropriate forum for redressing unjust actions, and rightly so. When the legal system is used to correct the mistakes made by haphazard management of dismissal or as a way to express the former employee's anger and frustration at having been dismissed, the costs of dismissal mount rapidly. Litigation devours precious company time and energy. It diverts company resources into both preoccupation with a possible settlement and reassignment of work to be done and project delays. This is not to suggest that companies should not terminate employees for fear of litigation. It merely suggests that care must be taken to protect the employment contracts and provisions of employment sanctioned by law. Many of the managers interviewed for this project have expressed dismay at the need to observe protective legislation mandates. The laws are often viewed as nuisances. However, if the safeguards are followed and become a routine part of dismissal management, companies need not live in fear of economic ruin through litigation. The laws encourage us to curb our own potential for abuse. While it is true that the legislation and its interpretation limits our freedom to act independently, it also causes us to evaluate our own actions in the light of potential repercussions.

Revenge Costs   Even if the price we may pay for unwise dismissals in legal actions does not encourage us to carefully review each dismissal, the likely revenge costs may catch our attention. Uncounted thousands upon thousands of dollars are lost each year in attempts by former employees to get back at employers who "have done them wrong." Most companies can cite at least one or more instances where former employees have stolen important documents, office property, poisoned the company image by leaking important information to competitors, threatened bodily harm to managers, or destroyed expensive company property. A major oil company was the object of a plot by three disgruntled former employees who planted bombs in the plant. To deal with this threat, the company was forced to shut down production for two days to locate the devices. Losses were calculated in the millions.

Other examples of revenge costs abound. Consider the fired employee of a seashell paving material firm who returned two days after he was terminated to bulldoze two buildings. Damages were assessed at $25,000. A security guard on the scene fled for his life. The former employee was held on $36,000 bond and charged with attempted murder, aggravated criminal damage, and criminal trespass.

Angry employees need to vent their anger through appropriate channels. Many times this is simply not possible, given the employee's psychological and emotional makeup. However, managers owe it to themselves to identify these potentially dangerous individuals and work with them before termination becomes necessary to short-circuit revenge actions that harm all concerned.

Personal Costs

The Human Resource Impact   In their best-selling book, *In Search of Excellence,* Peters and Waterman (1984) suggest that one of the significant characteristics of the competent company is its concern for the people who work for the organization. This concern for the human element is not solely related to the financial bottom line, although economic considerations cannot be ignored. Employees who remain will experience an adjustment period as they assess their own reactions to the dismissal and try to make sense of the action. Some employees who witness the leaving of another may become more careful of their own performance; others may express relief at the departure. One thing is certain: each will react to the situation based on the quality of their relationships with the terminee and the manager who terminates. Allegiance to the departing employee or loyalty to the manager may result in politically difficult relations in the work group. In some instances, reactions will vary from resentment to applause. Moving the workforce from preoccupation with the dismissal to a more normal work climate takes time and patience on the manager's part. The disruption effect may be brief or extended, depending on the reasons for dismissal and the manager's way of handling the discharge. At any rate, we must be aware of the potential effect of any dismissal on our employees' morale.

Managerial Stress Costs   Whether dismissals have been ordered from above to reduce costs or are an inevitable result of poor performance, each manager must consider how he or she will handle the actual dismissal. There is also a sense for us as managers that our necks are on the line. We may experience stress and a lack of confidence, mainly because it is not an action we perform often enough to become comfortable. Understandably, dismissal is also a process with which few of us *want* to become experienced.

Other by-products of dismissals—worry, loss of sleep, and preoccupation with the decision and the action—prevent us from maintaining our normal levels of productivity. Consequently our own job performance is likely to be affected by the contemplated dismissal. If the termination interview has not gone well, then the stress continues. Our own capacities for making mistakes may skyrocket if we feel frustrated by a termination.

The Employment Cycle

Just as crucial as recognizing why we should care how we conduct terminations is realizing that terminations are not isolated events with little relationship to our other employment monitoring duties. Hiring is inextricably linked to dismissal, as is performance appraisal. Figure 1-1 illustrates this relationship, showing how an employment cycle exists for each employee and each manager. It begins with the awareness of a job opening and evolves through dismissal. Most employees never experience the complete cycle, but are maintained in phases 6, 7, and 8. In examining the figure, dismissal should not be assumed as an automatic end result. it is merely one way to resolve dilemmas of performance.

The model is surrounded by a heavy dark line, symbolizing the context in which the cycle functions. This context could include economic factors contributing to layoffs, business decisions that eliminate some jobs while creating others, and other factors of the general business climate that can affect each company's personnel needs. Such external events may override the natural flow of the employment cycle.

When we find ourselves involved in a dismissal interview, we must be willing to question whether decisions we made in the hiring stage or actions we took (or failed to take) in the appraisal stage were contributing factors in each termination. The last portion of this chapter identifies problem areas in the selection interview and the performance appraisal interview that can reinforce judgment errors for managers.

The Selection Interview

Take a few moments to imagine the last person you interviewed for a position. How would you feel having to terminate this individual? The decisions we make in this setting may very well cast the die for this

Figure 1-1
The Employment Cycle

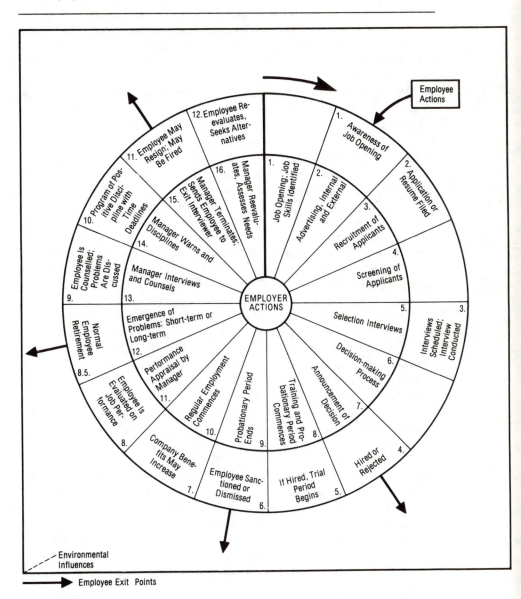

This model was developed by P. Michal-Johnson (1983).

person as an effective employee. Vague hiring criteria, rushing the interview, and stereotyping the person can spell trouble for the applicant and the manager. If we have hired, we will pay dearly for inappropriate decisions. We would all like to think of ourselves as totally rational beings, on the order of *Star Trek*'s Spock. The plain truth is that we are not. We are subject to the same weaknesses that have plagued humankind for an eternity. What are the trouble spots in selection interviews that generate bad decisions?

Management researchers have found two major errors in selection interviewing processes that result in poor hiring decisions. Both positive and negative stereotyping of applicants and allowing irrelevant factors to interfere with our perception of the applicant can spell trouble for the employment potential of any given applicant.

Stereotyping, or classifying people and situations into preordained categories, is a common but subtle part of the decision-making process. While it is illegal to allow race or sex to interfere in job selection, managers cannot easily divorce themselves from their own backgrounds, attitudes, and experiences. A manager who once was a poor struggling student cannot preferentially hire another based upon that similarity. In the same vein, we need not rule out applicants who do not fit into our personal preferences based on our own idiosyncratic rules of comfort. For example, a female supervisor ought not select only female applicants because she believes women are easier to work with.

As long as managers carry an image of the "ideal" employee into interviews, stereotyping will take place. Researchers Hakel and Dunnette suggested in 1970 that managers do in fact make decisions based on their own perceptions of what the ideal job candidate would be like. This does not mean that managers should not establish high ideals. Problems arise when the manager uses very narrow prescriptions, such as personality type, degrees from certain schools, and an applicant's connections to select employees.

Stereotyping raises a crucial dilemma for organizations. We know that hiring employees who can share core values and support the organization's culture can make for a stronger organization. Peters and Waterman (1984) tell us that the best companies are those that are guided by very strong values and have employees who abide by those values. Companies have the prerogative of hiring individuals who will fit in the organization. Recruiters and interviewers are interested in whether the person being screened will mesh into the chemistry of the department and the organization as a whole.

To ensure that you are functioning in a way that does not unfairly discriminate among job candidates, apply the following test. Write down those qualities you want to see in your employees in a column on the left-hand side of a sheet of paper. In the right-hand column identify key elements in the job description. As you look at the ideals, ask yourself whether your criteria will screen out people of a particular type. This exercise is not intended to discourage you from setting high standards for performance. Rather, it is intended to help you look for criteria unrelated to performance that you may be using in evaluating applicants.

In addition to stereotyping, other extraneous factors may creep into the evaluation decision and unfairly tip the scales in favor of a certain applicant. For example, whether the applicant sees us first or last or is sandwiched in the middle of the interviewing process may affect the decisions we make. If the interviews are all done in one day, as the day progresses we may grow bleary-eyed. The applicants all seem to run together and we may be biasing the last few interviews. Wallace, Crandall, and Fay (1982) also see the kind of information the applicant introduces and the timing of questions and responses as extraneous issues. For instance, the person who pauses to think about a question may be viewed as dull or slow, prejudicing the interviewer. If the interviewer is fatigued, in a hurry, or preoccupied, the accuracy of the interview decision is decreased.

What can we do to counteract these naturally occurring factors? First, we must pay attention to our silent criteria for hiring, the subtle characteristics that may unduly impress or distress us. Stewart and Cash (1982) tell us that we should increase the amount of time we allow the applicant to talk during the interview by asking more open-ended questions that are specifically directed toward job performance criteria, avoid making decisions early in the interview, and identify those employee characteristics that are most often related to success in the job for which the applicant is applying. During the interview we should probe for a match between the applicant and those important criteria.

It is to the applicant's advantage not to be hired for a job for which he or she is inappropriate. The critical incident approach offers one way of developing reasonable job-related criteria for measuring potential employees. The goal of this personnel process is to determine what specific aspects of the job are most critical to success or failure on the job. Question the top performers in your unit, asking them to detail exactly what they do in their jobs and how they do it. Ask the same question of your low-level performers, then compare the two lists. You should find some key differences, areas in which high-level performers function differently from their less successful counterparts. Work to translate those high-performance criteria into hiring goals for applicants. If we hire based on these successful characteristics, we may reduce the tendency to terminate because of poor hiring decisions.

Regardless of the fit, we must be aware of fair employment practices that prohibit arbitrary decisions in hiring, evaluation and promotion, and dismissal. Legal departments have already made us aware of these prohibitions. While the legislation and supporting executive orders may seem confusing and difficult to follow, it is every manager's job to be familiar with them. Some companies have become so afraid of the delicacy of this process that they have hired personnel consultants to take over their personnel functions entirely. The consulting organization then takes all the responsibility for implementing fair personnel processes.

Companies who choose this drastic leasing measure must be aware of the complications that may arise from such an arrangement. Consultants are unlikely to understand the company history well enough to appreciate the personal chemistry necessary to each work unit. Thus their hiring decisions are vulnerable to some of the same problems as internal hiring and employee monitoring. Leasing is a clinical answer to a problem that is often unpredictable because of the human factors involved.

At any rate, the fact that some organizations choose to lease a personnel agency to control hiring simply reinforces the importance of compliance with equal protection provisions. Equal protection procedures are important to consider throughout the employment cycle. They are important in the selection process as well as in appraisals of employee performance. The manager who fired a female employee with the justification, "it's about time you started having a family," (Alsop, 1980) learned the hard way. The woman sued, winning a $40,000 settlement, and the personnel administrator was fired. We owe it to ourselves to be aware of our legal responsibilities. A partial list of these requirements appears in Figure 1-2.

Bona fide occupational qualification (BFOQ) is a term to become aware of. It refers to the specific requirements of a job that mandate specific characteristics in an employee. While the Equal Employment Opportunity Commission warns us against hiring based on sex, color, creed, or national origin, there are certain times when any of these might be a BFOQ. For instance, it could be convincingly argued that an actor portraying Martin Luther King in a television movie should be both male and black. For stevedores it is important to be able to lift heavy crates, so the BFOQ of physical strength may disqualify certain individuals who could not match the needs of the job.

Legislation and executive orders prohibiting discrimination can make the selection interview perplexing. To assist in careful hiring conduct, the chart in Figure 1-3 clarifies some general areas to address and avoid in the selection interview. This list is by no means an exhaustive one, but provides a sense of key areas targeted by equal protection legislation.

Performance Appraisal Interviews

While it is true that not all dismissals are a result of performance problems, many are. When performance difficulties can be identified early on, it stands to reason that we have a better chance of rectifying them. Allowed to progress, the situation may fester, necessitating drastic actions like dismissal or transfer.

Figure 1-2
Key Laws to Consider in the Employment Cycle

AFFIRMATIVE ACTION

Executive Orders 11246 (1965) and 11375 (1967) establish the function of affirmative action in recruitment, employment, and promotion of groups that have been discriminated against in the marketplace. Affirmative action promotes fair treatment of individuals, demanding that employers and contractors who have contracts with the federal government in excess of $10,000 demonstrate they have made every effort to secure the employment and promotion of minority applicants based on an appropriate recruitment policy. If an employee can prove that termination resulted from discrimination because of race, color, religion, sex, or national origin, then litigation may ensue through Equal Employment Opportunity Commission (established by the Civil Rights Act of 1967). Documentation of complaints by employers is crucial should the employee file suit. Effective handling of the litigation issue is grounded in clear performance criteria, adequate advisement, and counseling, as well as appraisal. Employees must prove that they were not given sufficient opportunity to alter performance or behavior or were unaware of expectations of their manager.

HANDICAPPED EMPLOYEES

Section 503 of the Vocational Rehabilitation Act (1973) cautions employers to avoid actions that have an impact on handicapped employees. Terminations resulting from the handicap are subject to close scrutiny.

THE VIETNAM-ERA VETERANS READJUSTMENT ASSISTANCE ACT (1974)

This act follows the affirmative action executive orders in requiring that companies with federal contracts in excess of $10,000 recruit and advance qualified veterans disabled by the war.

SEXUAL HARASSMENT

In 1980, the Equal Employment Opportunity Commission took an unequivocal stand on compromising the employment of employees. Any action that interferes with an individual's job performance or "creates an intimidating, hostile, or offensive work environment" can be viewed as an illegal act.

Performance appraisals are receiving a lot of attention these days. A survey of *Training and Development Journal* readers indicated that about 65 percent train their managers to conduct performance appraisal interviews (Smith, 1984). We can assume that most companies, large and small, have developed some method to evaluate their employees.

Why Appraise Performance? Appraisals have been devised to measure performance, motivate employees, improve performance, plan

Figure 1-3
Interviewing with Caution

What You Can Ask		What You Cannot Ask
Applicant's address	—— but ——	Cannot be used to determine race, creed, color, or national origin
		Questions related to age
Criminal convictions	—— but ——	Arrests cannot be considered
		Birth certificate not allowed
Citizenship of applicant	—— but ——	Race must be ignored
Educational background		
Current salary		
Handicaps or disabilities that may be job-related	—— but ——	Cannot question how the handicap occurred
Health status		Marital status, Religion National origin
References		
Work experience		

Taken from Sincoff and Goyer (1984).

future work, teach employees what they should know, and distribute raises and promotions. Given their many functions, the appraisal systems in use have undergone dramatic revisions. Rating and ranking forms have changed from indicating grooming and hygiene to evaluating job performance.

Resnick and Mohrman (1982) suggest that the first step in planning performance appraisals is to determine the organization's reason for doing them. Wallace, Crandall, and Fay (1982) suggest there are three major reasons for implementing a performance appraisal system: (1) audit and control, (2) development, and (3) research. To discover what really happens in each department and job, as well as to manage all the job-related activities in a more desirable way, may be the goal of some companies. Others may view the appraisal process as a function of personnel development, an instrument for encouraging better performance.

Still other companies may give credence to the performance appraisal process because they find it provides them with valuable information or data that can be used to develop new programs, renew ongoing projects, and gain valuable input about employee attitudes toward the organization. In preparation for the next round of appraisals in your own shop, it might profit you to examine why appraisals occur in your workplace.

It may serve us well to discover what practitioners and researchers alike have to tell us about this type of interview, as we further develop our repertoire of management talent. One thing most people who work with appraisals can agree on is that some managers are likely to avoid or postpone them because they are difficult to implement. The difficulty arises because appraisals demand some form of judgment of the employee.

Common Problems Experienced in Appraisals   As early as 1965, Meyer, Kay, and French were considering the serious issues involved in performance appraisals. They told us:

- Criticism has a negative effect on the achievement of goals.
- Performance improves most when specific goals are established.
- Defensiveness resulting from critical appraisal produces inferior performance.
- Coaching should be a day-to-day, not once-a-year, activity.
- Mutual goal-setting, not criticism, improves performance.
- Interviews designed to improve performance should not weigh salary and promotion at the same time as performance.
- Employee participation in setting goals yields favorable results.

With these criteria in mind, it is easy to critique the systems we all use. A perfect system may not exist, but one thing is certain: any system is only as good as the manager using it. A district personnel officer for a large grocery chain said, "It's not the system we use that's the problem, it's getting our managers to use the system." Most managers who hesitate or postpone the interview say, "We're just too busy." Translated, it usually means, "I'd really rather not." Sound familiar?

Remember: the skill we demonstrate in the performance appraisal interview can reduce potential terminations and ease those we do conduct. Spending time earlier in the appraisal process can actually wind up saving us time if we find that we must terminate an employee.

Suggestions for Implementing Appraisals   Sportscasters often refer to team strategies in interviewing coaches who describe their game plans for upcoming athletic contests. Top-dollar athletes know the value of game plans, practice, and mental rehearsal before the event. Winning Olympic skiers Phil and Steve Mahre used mental rehearsal to prepare them for the dangers of icy and perilous skiing conditions. Managers can follow their lead. While termination is not a game and performance appraisals are not just key plays, it is foolish for managers to approach such a critical process without a reasonable strategy for implementing it.

Figure 1-4 offers a five-pronged approach to effective appraisals. The recommendations were taken from Patricia King's recent book *Performance Planning and Appraisal* (1984).

Figure 1-4
Effective Performance Appraisals

---

1. *The time and place of the appraisal is crucial.*
   - Privacy must be ensured. Use conference rooms where no interruptions will occur.

2. *Gathering accurate information for the appraisal is essential.*
   - Have all the pertinent records that chart success and failure on work projects.
   - Examine the person's job description to check that it accurately reflects work that is accomplished.
   - Observe the person's performance over time—not the week before the appraisal.
   - Avoid becoming side-tracked by minutiae—look for trends.
   - Call in others' opinions about the person's performance.

3. *Protect the employee from weaknesses in your own evaluation attitudes.*
   - Ask yourself how you rank people. Do you tend to rank and rate employees as a whole too high or too low—or as average?
   - Are you likely to blame a person's poor performance on his or her character? Always look for other explanations first.
   - Do you protect employees who try hard?
   - Are you likely to rate an employee higher or lower based on your perceptions of other strong or weak performers?

4. *Encourage the employee to develop a self-appraisal.*
   - The employee has much to contribute by way of placing issues in context.
   - Give the employee plenty of time to develop their own appraisals (at least a week).

5. *Plan the discussion with an agenda.*
   - Open the meeting by stating objectives and establishing an open tone to promote honest problem-solving.
   - Invite the employee to present the self-assessment.
   - React to the employee's self-assessment. Start with shared perceptions. Introduce questions of your own.
   - Study causes of any problems noted.
   - Establish goals and objectives and design a plan for the next appraisal period.

Communicating in the Appraisal Interview   The way we communicate with the employee is of prime importance in the appraisal interview. If we are too heavy-handed and critical, we jeopardize our potential effectiveness. If we are not straightforward enough about important issues we defeat our own purposes. Since the appraisal is a joint effort, use of plural pronouns like "we" when emphasizing problem-solving efforts usually produces more positive results.

> *"It seems to me* that you are saying you can't work efficiently when other employees are hovering around your desk. *How can we* rectify that situation?

Another tool that focuses on goals, not criticism, is the use of verbs that are less demanding. We might say, "I would like to see you . . ." instead of "I want you to . . ." Develop language whose sole goal it is to clarify problems and issues. Not "what are you going to do about it?" but "how can this issue be resolved?" Since the appraisal process is a sensitive one, words that signal defensiveness and demean the employee can generate unpleasant results. Defensive communication will be examined in greater depth in Chapter Six.

Which Employees Deserve Appraisal?   The carefully considered answer to this question is "all of them!" A myth common in management circles is that it makes more sense to follow the recommended procedures for appraisal only with professional or salaried employees who are better educated and represent the greater financial investment.

It is true that nonexempt or hourly workers hired at minimum wage are less influential or powerful, especially if they have no official representative. However, when employees are treated as wholesale goods or unskilled bodies filling job slots and are dismissed without regard to cause and due process, they become forces to reckon with. When a powerless group or individual becomes frustrated, the chances of revenge actions are likely to rise. The ill-advised dismissal without appraisals and appropriate consultation opens the door for employee morale problems— especially when others witness or discover the action.

A second aspect of this myth deserving illustration is the assumption that hourly workers are absolutely dispensible. Many of us, in our positions as managers, started out as hourly employees. By and large, many of the managers in grocery stores and other retail outlets began their careers stocking merchandise, running cash registers, or selling the goods of the company. It is not uncommon for secretaries to become office managers or for line workers to become supervisors. In fact it is part of the American Dream. To think that we need not take care to humanely advise these employees in the hourly job classifications is to suggest that we do not believe that some of our future managers are part of this workforce. When we fire without honest appraisal, we can set in motion a potentially counterproductive cycle of abuse. How? Most of us unconsciously model ourselves after those we observe in powerful positions—at least on some level. They may be teachers, managers, parents, and the like. If a manager fires hourly workers in flagrant disregard of legitimate and reasonable procedures, those who work for him or her may in time do the same.

Managers often appeal to time and profit to justify their failure to take the most just and reasonable approach to appraisal. The reasoning goes like this: "If we take the time to appraise employees we will lose money, because it takes so much time. If we carefully document appraisals, it keeps us from our work. We're not record-keepers; we're managers."

The answer to these arguments is relatively straightforward. When we ignore appraisal procedures, we invite poor performance and avoid corrective feedback. This in itself costs time and money in lost effort. If the situation escalates until we have to dismiss, we face all the costs noted at the beginning of this chapter. In the words of a popular television advertisement for preventive auto maintenance, "pay me now, or pay me later."

It is tempting for small business managers to forget the procedures and processes because it takes time to implement systems of appraisal. The mom-and-pop business operator may think, "well, it's just us, family." Eventually, however, we pay for our lack of care. We may pay through damage to our property and theft by a disgruntled employee; we may pay through diminished employee satisfaction; or we may pay in poor performance and retraining costs. Nonetheless, we pay. It is not just the educated professional who deserves care in this process, it is everyone in our employ.

More and more, the performance appraisal process is becoming an expected part of our supervisory responsibilities and our job descriptions as managers. Learning to conduct fair and helpful appraisals enhances our own marketability. How have we learned to conduct appraisals? Have we learned by watching our managers appraise our performance? Perhaps we have taken the examples we have seen as models. The factors we like least in our own bosses' handling of our performance appraisals may be sensitive areas in our own conduct of appraisals. If we resent being evaluated, are we likely to view appraisals of others favorably?

The performance appraisal interview can be a challenging opportunity for reevaluation and assistance for managers and employees, *if* we expect productive results. Furthermore, the appraisal process as a composite function involving counseling, goal-setting, or disciplining is the bridge between the selection and termination processes. Our abilities to diplomatically and honestly work with others to improve their working lot in the appraisal process will directly affect our ability to function well in the termination process.

Sir Isaac Newton postulated that for every action there is an equal and opposite reaction. This law also applies to the employment process. No action occurs in isolation. The skill we bring to selection interviews and performance appraisals enables us to initiate dismissals from a stronger and more sensible position.

SUMMARY

We must all be prepared for the costs of dismissal. When a termination is set into motion, a sensitive cycle is activated. Financial costs, in the form of turnover, litigation, and revenge actions, and personal costs involving human resource depletion and managerial stress complicate the issue. These costs should not discourage us from making decisions to dismiss, but they should remind us of the seriousness of the action. Likewise, in thinking of the employment cycle we should recognize that dismissals are not isolated acts but are related to other actions we have taken with the employees. Not surprisingly, dismissals are also related to actions the employees have taken with us. Both the selection interview and the performance appraisal interview present us with opportunities to improve our employment decisions. Suggestions for handling each type of interview can also prepare us for more effective management of dismissal interviews.

As we continue to consider whether to dismiss an employee, we owe ourselves, the employee, and the organization the obligation to fairly determine the risks of termination. In many instances we will proceed with the action and improve our working environment. When we have taken care in assessing the stakes of termination, it can pay off for us in the long run.

2

THE DISMISSAL INTERVIEW: ISSUES TO CONSIDER

While we have come a long way from the Ebeneezer Scrooge and Simon LeGree role models of firing, there is clearly room for improvement. For every fair and responsible dismissal there must be at least one other that violates a sense of justice and fairplay. Consider Bruce, a forty-four-year-old New Jersey engineer who went to his box to pick up his biweekly check. Attached to his pay envelope was a letter of termination instructing him to pack up his desk, go to personnel for severance processing, turn in his keys, and leave the premises. Employees confronted with situations like this have reason to complain about treatment and they do complain.

Understanding the Function of Dismissals

Is Dismissal a Legitimate Managerial Responsibility?

There is little doubt that terminations are an important part of managing the workforce. When Heizer (1976) asked managers to report the amount of time they spent recruiting, selecting, and terminating employees, all personnel issues, they suggested that 20 percent of their managing time was devoted to these activities. Terminations made up roughly half of that figure. What would account for this expenditure of time and energy in terminations?

First, these managers were not simply referring to the dismissal itself. Their estimate included time spent alone evaluating employee problems and in meetings with others contemplating termination actions—not to mention time spent examining files, developing cases to justify the action, warning the employee, and, finally, acting on the decision in the interview.

Second, action that is taken to discourage an employee from working for us—through transfers to other departments or resignation incentives—must also be considered as part of the dismissal process.

Many companies that would rather avoid the possibility of legal reprisals tend to export or transfer their problem performers to other departments or branch offices. Time spent in negotiating transfers can also count in Heizer's dismissal figures. At first glance, calling transfers dismissals may seem to beg the question. However, if we count departure as an involuntary act initiated by the manager to remove the person from the work group, the transfer takes on more of the characteristics of dismissal. We can think of the transfer as dismissal from one department and rehiring by another. In some cases the transfer is a move designed to encourage the employee to resign. Other resignation incentives may include demotion or job reassessment. In some Japanese companies, when an employee is no longer useful, he or she may be assigned to an office with no real work. While modern Japan increasingly terminates, the family model of traditional Japanese companies allows for this sort of isolation.

Can Fair Terminations Increase a Manager's Credibility?

Managers who terminate employees appropriately for failure to produce and for serious infractions may, in fact, have more productive work units. Failure to terminate can be more devastating than the actual termination—especially in the cases noted above. O'Reilly and Weitz (1980) studied marginal employees in a large retail sales organization and concluded that managers who employed sanctions, including terminations, had higher performing groups than those supervisors who took such actions infrequently. The moral of this study might be that managers who use terminations wisely and judiciously gain the respect of the remaining workforce. Employees are likely to understand that quality performance is expected.

What Makes Some Terminations More Difficult Than Others?

Inevitably, differences in personality, the reasons for the termination, and circumstances affecting the event will make some dismissals more difficult. When some fifty midwestern managers were asked to describe the differences between extremely difficult interviews and those that were tolerable, their answers suggested that difficult terminations occurred if they:

1. Were under heavy stress when they made the decision to terminate.
2. Found it hard to keep the interview on track because of the influence of the employee's communication.
3. Were rigid or unbending in the interview.
4. Were awkward and did not know what to say.

5. Dismissed the employee for poor interpersonal skills.
6. Viewed the employee as a poor listener.
7. As managers did not have a plan for the interview or abandoned the proposed plan.
8. Described the employee as disagreeable or unpleasant.
9. Failed to predict how the employee would react to the message of termination.

This study by Michal-Johnson (1981) supports the assumption that planning is an important part of the effective dismissal interview. If employees view the action as a necessary evil and expect the decision, the interview seems to be a formality. This awareness reminds us that in many cases the appraisal process establishes the rationale for termination.

How Well Prepared Is the Average Manager to Conduct Terminations?

Most managers in the study reported above said they learned how to fire employees strictly through on-the-job training. None had been through company programs to help them in the actual interview. Many companies offer intensive assistance with legal issues or examining company procedures, but not in the actual delivery of the dismissal.

A secondary issue related to how well managers conduct terminations brings up a confusing dilemma. When Stybel (1978) asked managers about how to conduct terminations, they had very strong opinions. However, when the actual behavior of the same individuals was observed, their opinions were not always reflected in practice. These managers were caught in the gap between ideals and action. Having a well-orchestrated plan of action is just as essential in the termination interview as in the appraisal process.

Organizational Philosophies of Dismissal

How Can We Discover Our Organization's Termination Philosophy?

In addition to considering the manager's role in termination, we must be aware that organizations, like people, also have their own attitudes toward termination. When we work for a company we are affected by the company philosophy.

Every business or profession conveys its philosophy in a variety of ways. To determine our company's approach, we look first at formal communication channels such as memoranda, newsletters, public statements, and annual reports. Through such documents we can discover how the organization says it sees itself.

We can also observe the communications of powerful figures in the organization and try to understand what they convey about the organization's self-image. In the abstract this concept, also known as the organization's metaphor, may be difficult to comprehend. But we may learn a lot from exploring the various metaphors in use in our company, as Koch and Deetz (1981) did in a study of organizations.

Some organizations function as large or small machines, as military units, as sports teams, as families, as fitness centers, or even as farms. The attitude displayed in these organizations directly affects the way terminations are viewed. Let us examine some of the these attitudes or philosophies in greater detail These attitudes may not be overtly recognized, but they are revealed through the actions taken in the organizations. To that extent, we can think of them as covert communications.

The Organization As Machine

When the organization functions as a machine, the parts of the organization are viewed as interchangeable. Consequently, no one is indispensable. When a machine breaks down it must be repaired and the broken parts are tossed out or scrapped. A second major part of the mechanistic view of organizations thus involves the maintenance of machinery. The organization will function best when there is a minimum amount of friction, but enough pressure to ensure quality output. The mechanically oriented organization may view the termination interview as a necessary maintenance action geared toward keeping the whole machine functioning.

While people are viewed as units of production and cogs in the wheels that turn the production flywheel, they are not treated as unique, creative beings. There is a master plan, a way that the machine is to be built. The mechanical organization may operate efficiently so long as human issues do not arise.

The Military Mind

An organizational philosophy that differs slightly from the machine metaphor is the military unit. Military organizations are likely to be governed by rules. Every action is by the book and power comes from the top. Decisions are made to be followed, not questioned. Those who violate rules are put in the brig (transferred to an undesirable position) or court-martialed and booted out. Tried and true processes are not tinkered with, rank has its privileges, and insubordination is not tolerated. Inspections are crucial to the military organization. The rituals, parade dress, and codes of conduct are carefully adhered to and sustain the system itself. The military organization may have a view of employees that is rigid or unbending. In the termination interview, the "recruit" or soldier is likely to be told what rules he or she broke and what the punishment will be. The dressing down of the soldier can be a part of the termination interview; typical accusations might include disloyalty or dishonor.

On the Playing Field

When the organization is the team, the goal of the work group is to win. To the team, "winning isn't everything—it's the only thing!" Vince Lombardi's quip reinforces the importance of playing as a unit. Nothing that is done encourages the maverick playing of individuals. The self-aggrandizing individual is likely to sit on the bench or punt. Managers may be subject to "pep talks" to get their players fired up for the big game (contract, etc.). But, as in sports, there are rules. For golfers, the out-of-bounds markers serve this function. For basketball players fouls are infractions; for football players there are yardage and possession penalties. In the termination interview of a team player, the employee may be accused of not giving 100%, not being in shape, not being fired up. The faltering employee may be told he or she has not made the cut and will be placed on waivers to function as a free agent. It also may be that another new player, a real blue-chipper, deserves a chance to show what he can do. The sports metaphor encourages the manager-coach to "put the other guy in."

A Family Affair

A Denver-based executive placement counselor told me of his work with a troubled family operation, where a blood-brother had to be fired. It was with great fear and concern that the company president phased out his brother's role in the company. If we fire our brothers, do they cease to be family? Many organizations are family-owned in real life; just as many take on the family metaphor. Not unlike the Japanese concept of company as family, employees are treated as brothers and sisters, sons and daughters for a lifetime arrangement. Once a member of the family, always a member of the family.

When a layoff is imminent, the family-like organization may choose to reduce everyone's work hours in order to ensure that no family member is expelled. Termination interviews involving managers and subordinates who function in this way are likely to be painful. While "father knows best," it is still difficult to have a child leave the fold. A termination is likely to produce the alienation or guilt-ridden response of the severed family relation. The terminee in the family is best compared with the disowned son or daughter, the black sheep.

The termination interview can actually take on the communication patterns of the stereotypical family. The manager may become paternalistic, saying, "This is really best for you," "This hurts me as much as it hurts you," "You have embarrassed the family," "We have told you and told you and told you." Because the ties between people may be closer in the family organization, employees who remain may feel that they have lost a brother or sister.

The Human Enterprise

Just as cartoonists frequently give inanimate objects human characteristics, creating talking washing machines and automobiles, we may unconsciously think of our organization as a living, breathing person. We may actually talk about the human attributes in casual conversation. The head, limbs, heart, and mind of the organization are clearly vital and essential elements to the survival of the personalized organization. In such an organization terminations may be seen as amputations or transplants. Statements like "engineering is the heart of this organization" describe the human organization. If it appears that one of the necessary parts of the anatomy is in danger of malfunction, critical resuscitation efforts may go into effect. Healing the ailing body is an important process to ensure continued health.

The Agricultural Enterprise

We have all watched a meticulous gardener caring for a crop. Whether it is by hoeing, spading, planting, weeding, thinning, reaping, or plowing, the gardener watches each process very closely, nurturing the ground at each stage. The organization that prunes away the underbrush so that the healthy plant can flourish is likely to view the termination as a necessary and expected process: "This is what we do to take care of the whole crop." If one person is holding the production group back, he or she may be pruned from the vine or merely transplanted to another environment that allows growth.

This view does not mean that remedial steps cannot be administered. Yet some plants can flourish only if transplanted to a sunnier spot with more irrigation and are unlikely to respond to attempts to eliminate troubling pests. In the gardener's world, survival of the fittest may be the law for plants that have been conscientiously cared for but are not capable of surviving.

Few organizations will spell out their actual philosophies of termination for us, but it can be helpful to discover if our own personal philosophies of termination are compatible with the dominant company attitude. For example, if we view the organization as an organic entity with its own personality, but those in power operate as though it is a machine, the gap may create some difficulty for the manager.

Why Employees Are Dismissed

"Because I said so." The answer parents give to curious children who constantly question parental requests is often a tempting response for managers. However tempting the answer, it is simply inadequate. Employees who are asked to leave deserve to know the reason behind the termination. We would expect that courtesy if our own jobs were on the line.

The cause for dismissal is an important variable in determining the most appropriate strategy to follow in the termination. A layoff is handled differently than a termination for theft; fighting deserves different treatment than does committing an expensive error caused by sloppy work habits. In 1972, Alfred Avins, dean of the Delaware Law School documented eleven different categories of misconduct for which employees can be dismissed for cause. The valid causes of termination include absence without leave, nonperformance of job duties, disobedience of orders, breaches of discipline, disrupting relations with coworkers, lying and falsification, theft, disloyalty and corruption, damage to property or goodwill, disabling conduct, and disreputable conduct outside the company.

The most common reasons cited by managers for dismissals are layoffs resulting from economic conditions and reorganization, violations of company rules, job incompetence, and interpersonal incompetence. It can be important to recognize that some terminations may develop from more than one of these factors. Interpersonal incompetence and violation of a company rule may provide a dual rationale for dismissal.

Layoffs

Layoffs can be viewed as either a temporary stop-gap or a permanent action. Companies may attempt to reduce their workforce by eliminating jobs across the board, by cutting special functions, or by shrinking the size of the rank-and-file labor force. Union contracts and provisions generally simplify the rank-and-file decisions, invoking seniority regulations, but at managerial levels the task is not so cut and dried.

An important factor in determining how layoffs will be implemented is the extent of the financial need. If management is protected from cuts and the streamlining avoids all levels, the credibility of the layoff will be viewed as suspect. Legitimate reductions in force take into account the inevitability of the action. In such instances, the whipping boy is no one but the accident of bad times. Being in the right place at the wrong time, fate, or even inappropriate decisions to expand can explain the need for the layoff.

Businesses nationwide have used the layoff as a means to cut out those employees they consider deadwood, soon-to-be pensioners, or hard to handle. Statistics cannot be offered to validate this practice, although many managers admit it has been done in their organizations. There is no way to prevent this miscarriage, but it should be viewed as a circumvention of the legitimate termination process. Companies who lay off the employee near retirement pay a price. When the word gets out that such practices are in vogue, potential employees will hesitate before applying and former employees may poison the waters of their new companies by telling horror stories about the old employer.

Violation of a Company Rule

Fraud, robbery, fighting, extortion, and sexual harassment are a few of the many major violations that may result not only in dismissal, but also in fines or prison sentences. While most terminations for rule violations are not so serious, they are one of the few ways companies have of enforcing the policies of the organization. Ignoring attendance policies, taking advantage of company privileges, or receiving inordinate numbers of personal phone calls on the job constitute some of these lesser infractions. The more serious violations generally do not call for prior warnings; they are part of what the company expects an employee would simply never do. Lower-order transgressions mandate warnings in appraisals. The result of continued abuses of the rules should also be clarified in the personnel manual, as well as in information given to newly hired employees.

With the first class of offenses, the need for counsel on legal ramifications is paramount. We need to know what our chances of success are likely to be if we decide to prosecute or sue for damages and restitution. When the charges against the employee are of this type, greater care must be taken than in traditional lower-order violations.

Job Incompetence

While most of us might think that dismissals occur mainly because employees cannot do their jobs well, the facts do not tend to bear this out. A proportionately higher number of employees are terminated because of rule violations or because they do not function well within the work group. Except in cases of gross violations, proving job incompetence may be difficult. If, for example, a bulldozer operator comes to work with a severe hangover and operates the equipment carelessly, endangering the lives of his coworkers, is that job incompetence or violation of a company rule? When a newly hired employee has difficulty learning the company's use of the computer terminals after two weeks, is that job incompetence or poor training? When we think an employee is "not doing his job," we must ask ourselves whether the job description is explicit enough and if we have clarified the nature of the job sufficiently to the employee.

The more vague the job description, the more difficult the termination interview for job incompetence. The burden of proof is clearly on us as managers to document the specific instances that constitute poor performance. This issue of incompetence must have been addressed in previous performance appraisals, giving the employee sufficient time to improve. A program of progressive discipline serves to put the employee on notice that he or she must clearly shape up or ship out.

A recent Dallas, Texas, case dramatized the issue of job incompetence. In this case, public outcry resulted in the termination of a nurse who screened emergency calls for ambulance service. The nurse, after being told that the victim could not talk to her, repeatedly demanded to speak to the victim, delaying the dispatch of the ambulance. The victim died before the emergency medical team arrived. Such obstructive behavior seemed unfitting and appeared to endanger lives of others in the community. Several questions arise from situations like this: Are the procedures governing the nurse's job explicit enough to clearly interpret her actions as procedural violations? Is this behavior a question of inappropriate social skills and immaturity?

Interpersonal Incompetence

We walk a very fine line when we dismiss employees because they simply cannot get along with others. While we can argue that most tasks carry the unwritten assumption that the individual will get along with customers and coworkers, it is awkward to prove unless the requirement has been included in the job description. As with other criteria for effective job performance, determining that an individual is not competent in relationships with others opens the door to subjective value judgments.

If a custom cabinet-building firm sends a representative into homes to measure kitchen walls and the employee barges into the home, insulting or offending the customer, is this grounds for termination? Bad impressions can lead to irritated customers and lost contracts, endangering the reputation of the company. Would you terminate? If so, on what grounds? Generalized statements about inappropriate behavior are not sufficient to warrant termination. We must be willing to clarify exactly what behaviors have created problems for us. Vague references to general incidents and tendencies will not suffice. This means documentation must be careful, with specific instances noted and warnings to the employee recorded.

We all find that we work best with some and worse with others. Fred Fiedler, a leadership expert, developed a rating scale for the Least Preferred Coworker—assuming that everyone has one. While it is more difficult for us to get along with some subordinates than others, simply having this difficulty because of general personality preferences cannot serve as a legitimate reason for termination.

The problems of preference for some rather than others presents a difficult dilemma for managers. We must guard against making ironclad evaluations of employee personality types, essentially reserving judgment. Managers who were interviewed by the author to discover examples of terminations for interpersonal incompetence said they had probably fired people simply because they did not like them. The typical scenario went like this: When the manager became disenchanted with the employee, he or she noticed every little irritating behavior. Then, once the employee was viewed as obnoxious or troublesome, in daily interactions and in appraisals, the manager could find nothing about the employee's performance that was up to par. Self-fulfilling prophecies like these can generate problem performances in and of themselves. To avert situations like this, third-party intervention is advisable. Bringing in our supervisors to observe the documentation and to monitor the action can serve as an important safety valve in dismissal for interpersonal incompetence.

A particular type of interpersonal incompetence, seen in employees of all ages, is immaturity. When an employee has great difficulty accepting criticism, tends to blame others, and fails to take responsibility for his or her own actions, the working relationship suffers. It is important for us to note that this condition is not the exclusive property of subordinates. Most of us on the other side of the desk are also prey to this disease. A key function of maturity is the ability to accept one's strengths and shortcomings, then strive to maximize the strengths and minimize the shortcomings. When interpersonal incompetence is based on immature behavior, documentation is critically important and interviews are likely to produce argument from the employee.

What Happens with Troublesome Terminations?

Even though we may follow the best-recommended path for conducting termination interviews, there is no way to ensure success. Following the recommended procedures, taking the event seriously, and cautiously communicating the dismissal reduce the potential of legal suit, but cannot completely eliminate the possibility. When a termination is not accepted by the employee and he or she challenges the decision, several means of remediation are available to the manager.

First, company policies for filing grievances can be utilized. Where union grievance conditions are well known, the individual may pursue a challenge with the help of a union steward. At any rate, these grievance procedures offer some structure for managers and employees to function within. In small companies, the grievance procedure may be handled more informally, which can make the challenge more difficult to handle.

Coulson (1981), an arbitration advocate, recommends a six-step grievance strategy to serve as a safety net for problem terminations.* Coulson favors third-party interventions to settle dismissal disputes.

1. The employee airs the complaint with the supervisor.

2. The supervisor responds within a few working days.

3. If the response does not settle the dispute, then the employee should have the right to appeal to the personnel manager. After consultation with the personnel manager and the department head, the written management decision should be submitted to the employee within three working days.

4. If the dispute still exists, the employee may appeal to the chief executive officer or submit to impartial arbitration. Professional arbitrators, at the employer's expense, can be assigned by the American Arbitration Association.

5. In arbitration, the employee has a representative and the company may have one. The arbitrator provides a decision after two to three working days.

6. Employees who have been unfairly discharged rarely wish to return to the company but favor financial settlement.

Arbitration is presented in Coulson's *Termination Handbook* as a reasonable alternative for companies who wish to avoid possible legal action. It offers certain advantages in terms of cost, time, and immediacy. With arbitration, many of the nuisance cases now on the dockets could have been avoided. When a Washington symphony orchestra member filed a sex discrimination suit against the orchestra challenging her dismissal, the judge was incensed. She was fired because of tardiness or absence in rehearsals, not because she was a woman. Legal suits generated out of anger might be most amenable to arbitration.

The arbitration process offers an additional advantage to the organization, in that it offers some protection to the company when poor termination decisions have been made. This form of redress has positive image value and can serve to boost morale. It also shifts the burden of the

---

*These arbitration procedures are most likely to be used with nonexempt employees.

decision to someone who has nothing to gain by choosing for either the company or its employee.

The obvious second alternative is to allow the situation to deteriorate to such a point that the disgruntled employee will do one of two things: either sue or drop the issue. Most companies hang in the balance, hoping the employee will forget about legal redress. It is a gamble. The difference between the two approaches, arbitration and legal suit, is a difference in style. Arbitration takes a proactive or positive stand, while passively waiting for the employee to act is clearly reactive. In football games we might call arbitration an offensive strategy while legal redress is a defensive strategy.

A Checklist for Managing Dismissals

Based on the writings of experts, interviews with countless managers, and the testimony of those who have been fired, the following suggestions identify some of the most critical considerations we must take into account when we are preparing to terminate. While we must judge each case according to its own merits, these recommendations can serve as guidelines.

1. Termination interviews must be conducted in a private setting. If you do not have an office, find a vacant room. Under no circumstances should the dismissal be handled in public around other employees.

2. Discover whether you are terminating the person on a holiday, birthday, or anniversary. Application files will have some of this information. Especially avoid Christmas and New Year's day firings. In cases of serious violations, this may be ignored, but only when the company safety is at stake.

3. Dismissals should be avoided on Friday afternoons. The employee terminated late Friday afternoon has the entire weekend to become upset. Termination interviews should be scheduled instead early in the week so the person can begin to think about applying for another job.

4. Double check the frequency with which you counseled, warned, and evaluated the employee. Be sure you have recorded and documented each instance. Include dates and times and take clear notes immediately after each incident. Ask the employee to sign off on each instance of warning, simply to note that they have heard the message. They need not agree with the warning.

5. Do not allow poor performers to drag on. Failure to terminate the marginal employee sanctions ineffectiveness and gives the person false hopes.

6. Were the job performance expectations and importance of compliance with company procedures clarified when the employee was hired?

7. In making the decision to terminate, did you use only firsthand observed evidence?

8. Plan the interview, including the opening, the middle, and the closing.

9. Recognize your own experience or lack thereof. If you are unsure, ask for expert help. It is worth it to you and to your organization.

10. Your personal goal in the termination process is to remain calm, regardless of what the other person does. If you are vulnerable to the employee's behavior, the plan you developed can easily deteriorate.

11. Identify the specific actions and behaviors that necessitate the termination. Honesty will be respected; placating will not.

12. Encourage terminees to talk to you. Let them know you want them to understand the action and feel they deserve straightforward treatment.

13. Assess whether the person you are terminating can endanger you or your organization through reprisal. If you do not trust the employee to leave peacefully, request security support. We must be aware when the employee has access to sensitive documents and equipment and can endanger or destroy them.

14. Anticipate as many reactions to termination as possible, remembering who the terminee is. Prepare yourself for loud outbursts, arguments, silence, tears, and disbelief.

15. Never terminate anyone on the phone or with a pink slip in the pay envelope.

16. Treat the person who is losing the job with dignity, *even though they may not be able to reciprocate!*

17. Avoid talking about how miserable you feel during the interview; this will be received as hypocrisy (except perhaps in layoffs).

18. Do not offer the person advice on how to handle this by trying to outline what he or she should do. This task belongs to someone else; it cannot be perceived as an honest attempt to help.

19. Keep the interview short. Long drawn-out termination interviews prolong the agony and pain for both parties involved. Avoid telling empathetic stories or quoting from personal experience.

20. Carefully evaluate the advisability of terminating; have you honestly explored other ways out?

Chances are this information is much easier to read than to practice. Our own styles of coping with terminations, our relationship with the employee through the appraisal process, and the reasons for the termination all complicate the process. In the following chapter, we will examine some of the more prevalent reasons why terminations can become difficult for managers and employees.

Are You Ready to Conduct a Termination Interview?

There comes a time when you feel there is simply no turning back. You must act in order to preserve your own integrity and that of the company. Even though you may feel that the time is right and you should strike while your iron is hot, *stop!* Before you embark on an interview that will affect you, your work group, and other employees, ask yourself these questions.

1. Have I made my expectations clear to the employee? How have I done it? In writing? Orally? How many times? Has there been sufficient and reasonable time for improvement? (Look at this question again! Are you really being honest?) Have I given the person a time frame for improvement?

2. Have I talked this issue over with my supervisor and the personnel officer involved? (Be sure you have a second opinion that is verified. It doesn't hurt to have this in your files.)

3. What do I have to know before I can begin to plan the termination process?

   a. What is the specific cause of this termination?

   b. Is this action based on one instance or a series of instances?

   c. Is this termination consistent with other firings in my company for similar offenses? Are all employees aware that an act like the one just cited will result in termination?

   d. Does this termination bear any resemblance to other terminations I have conducted?

   e. What sort of reaction can I expect from this specific person— based on my working relationship and my own assessment of him/her as a human being?

f. What do I honestly expect my own reaction to firing the person will be? During the interview? After the interview?

g. Do I have the experience and understanding of this person to conduct the interview by myself? Should there be a third party present? If so, who? What sort of support can I receive from this person? Why is he/she my choice?

h. Do I have a file established for this person including all performance appraisals, any notes from conferences, signed statements indicating the employee is aware of the issues?

i. Do I know what sort of severance package will be awarded? Is this package fair?

j. Can I offer this person outplacement counseling, or at the very minimum an exit interview with a staff termination counselor?

k. How soon will I want this person to leave? Why?

4. In the termination interview, how will I communicate the message? What is my strategy or game plan?

5. How will I begin the interview? What will I say and do?

6. How will I remind myself that I must follow these steps and cover this material? Notecards? Nothing?

7. How do I feel about terminating this person?
   Awful?   Glad?   Excited?   Guilty?

8. How do I feel about terminating in general?

9. Am I contemplating this action because *I* can't handle relating to this person any longer or because the employee is not making the kind of contribution the company deserves?

10. Is this termination my way of problem-solving? Is it an opportunity to get rid of the problem so I will not have to face my own deficiencies as a manager? What have I learned about my own skills as a result of this experience? (Don't fool yourself. Though this is the last of these questions, it may be one of the most important!)

SUMMARY

We are reminded that dismissal is a key responsibility of managers; that reasonable terminations actually enhance the manager's credibility; that difficult terminations seem to have certain common elements; and that managers, by and large, are not trained to cope with dismissals. All these observations help us to understand the function of dismissal in the organization. Another way of placing our company's policies and attitudes toward dismissal in perspective involves discovering the specific metaphor or culture around which the company functions.

Often the cause for a specific dismissal mandates the way the termination interview can be conducted. Whether the person is discharged because of company economics, a rule violation, or for job or interpersonal incompetence, the interview of dismissal will be affected.

The last three sections of this chapter offer suggestions for working with challenged dismissals through mediation or arbitration and checklists for handling actual terminations. With these considerations in mind, we are now ready to examine the interview itself in greater detail.

3

COMMUNICATING THE DIFFICULT MESSAGE OF TERMINATION

Communicating difficult messages is one of the major challenges we all face in the process of living. Generally we consider messages difficult when we are concerned they will disappoint others, cause them pain and suffering, promote guilt in ourselves, or play into our fears that we cannot handle the repercussions. There is no question that termination messages fit into this category. As you read this chapter pay particular attention to your own ability to send and receive difficult messages. You may not be as inexperienced as you think.

This chapter will assist you to prepare for a termination and analyze the situation. It suggests specific strategies for approaching various types of termination interviews, based on the cause for dismissal and your relationship with the employee, and lists the essential steps in the termination interview.

Developing the Dismissal Strategy

The cause of the termination can assist us in determining the most effective approach to take. For example, the sabotage of computer programs is certainly more dangerous than failure to punch a time clock properly; stealing from cash registers is more serious than failing to file reports. The nature of the cause foreshadows many of the reactions anticipated in the interview. We also feel differently about the infractions, which means that we will treat them differently. Although cause is not the sole predictor of outcomes in dismissal interviews, it is certainly an important one.

The major causes for termination are reiterated below. With each type, specific cautions and suggestions are offered to place the event in perspective. Again, the primary causes for firings are: economic conditions (layoffs), job incompetence, interpersonal incompetence, and violation of company rules or laws.

Economic Conditions (Layoffs)

In difficult economic times, we are often faced with the need to reduce staff or, in the extreme, to close our businesses. While these are not ideal options, at times they are the only realistic options available to us. It must be clear from the outset in cases of layoff that the sole motivating factor for the reduction in staff is economic.

When large numbers of employees are to be laid off, it is important to avoid mass announcements of the decision. Consultants typically recommend a phase-down approach to acquaint employees with the economic picture. Companies who herd their employees through rushed closings and render the decision in the form of pink slips may find sabotage and bad publicity to be more likely. It is important for each employee's supervisor to talk through the issue with the employee, since there is a bond already established. At the very minimum, private or small group interviews provide a safer setting for employee reactions. The small group interview also has the advantage of emphasizing that no one has been singled out.

Terminations by layoff should include the following steps:

1. Clarify the company's need to reduce the work force.
2. At least two months before the target date for staff reduction, inform employees of the potential reduction in force.
3. Identify the care that went into the making of the decision.
4. Label the layoffs as a last-ditch effort to save the company.

5. Stress that the decision cannot be interpreted as an evaluation of the employees' worth.
6. Clarify the basis for each employee's selection as one to be severed.
7. Make recommendation letters available to all employees, noting their loyal service and valued skills.
8. Notify them of job sources in the community.
9. Give them their survival package (described below).
10. State your willingness to support them as best you can.

The list of companies laying employees off is great. Many of those have a very difficult time assisting employees in this readjustment because everyone is readjusting, including the managers directing the layoff. Layoffs discourage direct confrontation. Again, however, the manager should lay aside his or her own pain and put the others first. It might seem easier to simply tell employees not to show up the next day and to apply for unemployment compensation. But this approach unleashes former employees who are essentially walking time bombs upon their families and friends and society at large.

The layoff can be handled intelligently or it can be a travesty. The decision depends on the length of time available for the staff reduction, the financial resources available, and the managerial philosophy of the company. The federal government has paved the way for private enterprise by establishing model programs for reduction in force. In a department of personnel management when reductions were mandated, career counseling and training in resumé preparation and interviewing skills were made available. Job banks were created for both government and private sector jobs. Actions like these serve to preserve the reputation of the organization. In the event that economic conditions improve, warranting additional hiring, former employees will feel better about returning.

The issues for the employee who is laid off will be adjusting to the situation and resurrecting job search skills. The employee who has worked in the same company for ten years is sadly out of touch. In some fields undergoing rapid technological development, there may not be any real future in their jobs. In such cases the availability of retraining is crucial. The worker must know that the world will go on, even though life may be substantially more difficult during the adaptation period. Organizations must encourage flexible thinking by presenting the alternatives available to the workers.

The new class of the unemployed are proud individuals who find it extremely difficult to accept government aid and will do virtually anything to remain independent of government "charity." Businesses can assist the employees in their resettling with the introduction of a survival kit. The survival kit includes information about applying for temporary unemployment insurance to help tide them over. The information should be framed as positively as possible, focusing on the temporary nature of the situation. The benefits the employee is entitled to must be explicitly set forth without jargon. Severance benefits must be clearly spelled out. According to Baytos (1979), companies may choose to continue hospitalization and other insurance policies for a reasonable period of time in lieu of providing wage or salary benefits. A reemployment module in workbook fashion can be included in the package that will allow the employee to start on the path of career change, industry change, or relocation. Suggestions about how and where to begin the job search in each particular industry can be extremely helpful to the employee whose world appears to have caved in.

Establishing an office to counsel the laid-off employee at another facility, maximizing union assistance, and offering names of local mental health counselors who charge on a sliding scale can be helpful as well. Encouraging groups of laid-off workers to meet regularly to discuss their situation and their progress can serve as a lifeline, keeping the employees from the isolation that promotes withdrawal and depression. Such groups can be led quite capably by lay persons from the group itself. The leader does have to stimulate the courage and imaginations of the workers. One such group in Houston, Texas has been formed to assist terminated employees over forty who have held managerial positions. For many this is the first time in their lives they have been without work. Their financial needs are quite high, as are their fear levels. The Forty Club, as it is called, encourages the rekindling of self-confidence, which is essential for job hunting. The participants are stimulated to view unemployment as a time to rediscover themselves, branch out, and generally learn to cope with adversity. The group reminds them of their wealth of experience and skills and helps in repackaging them. The success rate of the group is impressive. In fact, it keeps a winner's board with photos of successful graduates of the program.

Job Incompetence

In some ways, incompetence is more difficult to confront than layoffs. Dismissals due to economic conditions are justified as "acts of God" by management. The poor performance of a job is a very different matter. When we dismiss for job incompetence we are calling into question the skills, abilities, and judgment of the employee. Thus we must be able to validate our perceptions of incompetent performance. Evidence must be clear and well documented. Clear job descriptions and evaluation criteria make this aspect of the termination more manageable for both manager and employee (see Figures 3-1 and 3-2). When we have complied with

Figure 3-1
Aggressive Positive Discipline Approach

TO: Western Production Division   DATE: December 21, 1984
FOR: Carol Thompson
FROM: Carley Washington
RE: *Unsatisfactory Job Performance*

This letter is being written as a follow up to our meeting last Thursday, December 16th, at which time I informed you of my dissatisfaction with your performance on secretarial work in the Administrative Department.

The specific areas of unsatisfactory performance that were discussed were excessive turn-around time on various reports such as Sundry Notices, AFEs, Supplemental AFEs, Completion Reports, APDs, Purchase Orders and Purchase Requisitions, Warehouse Stock Lists, and various other miscellaneous reports. In many cases the turn-around time was 5–14 days and in some cases it was as long as three weeks.

Prior to our discussion last week, you will recall that you and I have had several conferences related to your work and the problems involved in getting the work processed in a timely manner. Also, on several occasions I farmed out some of the report typing to other secretaries in an effort to get you current on day-to-day work.

At the conclusion of our meeting last week, I informed you that I would provide you with a time schedule for completion of secretarial work on specific reports which, if accomplished, would constitute satisfactory performance. Attached is a separate schedule covering the majority of the day-to-day work assignments.

Satisfactory performance also includes timely mailing of daily reports and correct distribution of same without the need for individual instructions.

At the conclusion of two work weeks, January 4, 1985, you and I will review your performance for that period of time to determine if your work is being done within the time frames indicated. Any unusual circumstances that may occur which would affect your achieving the goals set out will be taken into consideration. If your work is still unacceptable, you will be given another two weeks work opportunity (January 21, 1985), to correct the situation at which time a review will occur and determination made regarding your future employment opportunity.

Carley Washington

CW/cb
CC: Bob Barrow

Figure 3-2
Typing Requirements

Regulatory Function

One day turn-around on the following:

1. TWXs
2. First Delivery Sundry
3. Budget Status Report
4. Monthly Report of Wells Completed
5. Memos as instructed

Three-day turn-around on all remaining requested routine typing.

Large work projects and high-priority reports will be handled on an individual basis under the supervision of the Department Supervisor.

Purchasing and Materials Function

Two day turn-around on the following:

1. One page P.O.s
2. Automobile Requisitions
3. Automobile Change Forms
4. On-Hand-On-Order Reports
5. Request to Issue Master Work Contract
6. Office Supply Requisitions
7. Memos (one-two days)

One-week turn-around on the following:

1. Multipage P.O.s—These types of P.O.s for wellhead-production equipment can be placed on Wang.
2. Inventory Listing

---

performance appraisal processes, issued warnings, and documented them, our task is less subject to cries of capriciousness and unfair treatment. In addition, the employee may be able to see the writing on the wall and resign rather than face dismissal.

Difficulties will arise when job expectations are not clear and our problems with employee's performance are not carefully documented. Managers have the right to establish the working contract, including all job criteria. To dismiss based on failure to comply with these criteria is a managerial responsibility.

The critical elements in the termination process based on job incompetence are:

1. Documented proof of the employee's inability to function in the job at the desired level of proficiency.

2. Evidence of managerial attempts to redress the problems. (See the aggressive positive discipline approach used by a manager of a clerical employee in Figure 3-1). The evidence may take the form of a letter or memorandum to the employee, summarizing the management effort to promote better performance.

In Figures 3-1 and 3-2, both the memorandum and the typing requirements specify the manager's expectations. Such documents, while not foolproof, help to clarify the degree of deviation that the manager will tolerate in performance. Not all jobs are as easily detailed as the position in the example, but attempting to clarify job requirements can reduce the latitude that we as managers have for making errors in dismissals for job incompetence.

Interpersonal Incompetence

When we terminate because the employee has trouble getting along with other employees, relating to customers, or coping with the natural and expected crises of the business world, we enter a delicate sphere. Since most job descriptions do not encompass such skills, we must rely on observations and developing conditions that serve as indicators that the employee is having a difficult time functioning as a positive team member. An employee who consistently promotes rumors about other employees, undermining worker morale, or one who loses his or her temper at the slightest provocation can be dismissed.

In each of these instances, the important element is managerial counseling of the employee regarding the desired behaviors and the problems that current behavior promotes. If the employee is one who we personally have difficulty tolerating, we must reexamine our own motives. Our relationship with the employee is clearly a two-way street. We must be sure that we have given the person the benefit of the doubt. It is possible that we are part of the problem.

A host of outplacement counselors have indicated that most managerial terminations, especially in the higher echelons of corporate life, result from problems of personal chemistry. If the work climate is not a comfortable or effective one, it may be traced to personality clashes and personal style differences. This lack of fit, in some instances, says little about the competency of the individual, but says a great deal about the tone of the managing circle with whom the person must function.

To prepare for the dimissal based on the interpersonal incompetence, we must recognize that the issues involved must be treated as objectively as possible. The difficulties can be clarified and identified. The results of the difficult communication interactions can be documented.

A second consideration is the nature of the issues involved in interpersonal incompetence. Such charges are delicate because we are spotlighting an intensely personal side of the employee's behavior. It is one thing to admit I don't know how to run a fork lift; another to suggest that I cannot control myself, adapt to other personalities, or share. The nature of the human animal is evident in this type of termination. As a result it is potentially volatile, especially if the employee fails to recognize these human relations problems. If as an employee I am blind to my own weaknesses, it may come as a great surprise to me that I am even talking with my manager about such personal behaviors.

When terminating for interpersonal behavior problems, we must expect defensiveness to surface in one way or another. Employees are likely to compare themselves with others, try to justify their behavior as someone else's fault, or verbally attack the manager's own abilities.

Violation of a Company Rule

There are rules and then there are Rules. One company may have a rule about punctuality that can be broken so long as the employee makes up the time. Another company may use the timeclock as its way of regulating an assembly line. The rules are essentially the same, but in one company violation is overlooked; in the other it is grounds for termination. Rules vary in stringency and penalty. Violations that reflect illegalities are likely to be taken more seriously than lesser infractions. Again, much of the interpretation of rules depends on the company philosophy toward procedures and rules. If we work in organizations that have clearly understood penalties for certain types of violations, it is easier to reprimand or dismiss based on such infractions. To some extent a strict statement of penalties relieves managers of the responsibility for making decisions on a case-by-case basis.

In dismissals for a rule violation, an important criterion is equity. Is the person receiving the same or an equivalent punishment as other employees for an equivalent infraction? We open ourselves up for undue criticism if we administer the procedures selectively. As with job incompetence, the termination is likely to proceed more smoothly if we have clearly identified the company's expectations for employee performance. Routine violations that are easily documented, like tardiness, often lead to cut-and-dried dismissals. As the violation becomes more severe, the interview often develops more complexity.

If the infraction involves damage to property or persons, the interview must be carefully controlled. Witnesses are essential; restraint can be necessary. If the violation is of a sensitive nature, be prepared to avoid unnecessarily loaded language in describing the incident. Each case must be judged on its own merit, taking into account the nature of the violation and how the violation is interpreted by you and your organization.

Never engage in verbal battles with the terminee accused of criminal offenses. Reiterate your own position after clearly citing the charges and clarifying them. These may include an explanation of company policies, referring to book, chapter, and verse. If a crime has been committed, you may want to involve the local authorities. On the other hand, in cases where your company would choose not to prosecute, simply let the person know that prosecution is an option that the company is considering. If the accused party has been apprehended and the offense warrants immediate removal from the work environment, safety precautions should be taken. Access to files, the person's office, and the cash register or post must be halted. The person should be allowed to claim personal effects, although it is best to have a security person or fellow manager retrieve them for the suspect.

Less stringent precautions are required for lesser violations, since the motivation producing the infraction is generally not malicious. Because of the difference in intensity, the nature of the messages sent under each condition naturally varies. In the latter case, the individual should clearly be told something like, "We must talk about the job you have done for us. In previous meetings with you it seemed quite clear that you agreed not to violate the vacation policy. This record indicates that you chose not to return to work on Friday, but on Monday."

Assessing the Nature of the Supervisor-Subordinate Relationship

While we must realize that communicating in the dimissal interview is not an exact science, because of all the variables involved, we can investigate the major factors involved. As discussed above, we can understand how employees have responded in the past and we can clarify the cause for dismissal. We turn now to the third major factor: the nature of our relationship with the employee.

Dismissal encounters will differ based on the nature of our relationship with the person to be terminated, the reason for termination, and the employee's reaction to the dismissal. Each termination is unique because these three variables cannot be identical. To illustrate the unique nature of each termination process, let us consider two cases involving different reasons for termination, two different employee reactions, and two different relationships between manager and subordinate.

CASE ONE: I have hired a retarded twenty-five-year-old man to assist in the food services department as a tray carrier in our hospital. After a week the staff has noticed that the man has difficulty relating to the patients and visitors. He is abrupt with them, becomes frustrated easily when they direct him to the desired table, and has a high number of food spills. After talking with him about these problems, I clarify exactly what it is that he must do when he carries patient and visitors' trays to their desired table. He is told that he has a week to learn how to improve his performance. If, after that time, there is no improvement, then he will be dismissed. He continues to work but there is no noticeable improvement. He must be terminated because of job incompetence. His primary response to difficult situations is confusion and frustration, manifested by simple repetition of phrases like, "I've tried."

Our relationship is still in the trial stage. I have made no major commitment to the young man. He has few expectations about this job being the ideal position for him. It is a job. I do feel awkward about the situation because he is severely handicapped. However, it is easier to confront the employee-job fit now than to allow it to go unnoticed. The termination interview is straightforward. I take him aside into the office and remind him that a week's time has passed. We talk about the problems that were mentioned the last time we talked and note the lack of improvement. He says, "I'm sorry. I tried." I have to tell him that we must have tray carriers who need little supervision and we feel that he will find a job that is better suited to his talents.

CASE TWO: Marilyn has worked in my office for five years as head book-keeper. She is knowledgeable and reliable. We have all learned to trust her. She is efficient and cheerful. None of the partners in the office particularly cares about the accounting process and entrusts most decisions regarding accounting to her. Several irregularities have cropped up recently. Receipts that normally would go to Marilyn are routed to the partners by new clients. There is a significant difference between the wholesale prices listed on the receipts and the prices we have set for the goods. The receipt prices are lower. We ask Marilyn to come into the main office to explain the disparities. She becomes flustered and says she doesn't understand the mistake. As we press her for the answer to the discrepancy, she breaks down and begins to cry. Slowly the pieces fit together. Marilyn has made informal agreements with clients to give them breaks on volume purchases if they make contributions to her. Suddenly a situation that began as a problem-solving effort becomes a dismissal interview. She has admitted to bribery, clearly a violation of a company rule as well as a legal infraction.

She is embarrassed and humiliated. She wants to escape this situation. She wants to know if we will press charges. Can she pay the money back? The dismissal becomes more complicated because of the history and the relationship we have all developed with her. We have long since passed through the trial or probationary stages; she has been accepted as part of the organization. Yet this act of dishonesty violates the trust we have placed in her and creates an unbridgeable credibility gap. We are all disillusioned and want to proceed to termination with all due speed.

Over time, Marilyn has developed a trusting relationship with the rest of the office. She has passed through the bonding stage with us. But at some point, she began to think in terms of a "me versus them" position regarding resources. This placed her in a differentiating stage. She could no longer honestly reveal her activities, necessitating more caution with her bosses. At this point there is no going back. It would be impossible for her to expect the partners to trust her again.

The termination message is one that signals disappointment in the development, terminates immediately, and calls for an audit to determine the amount of restitution.

Considering both of the cases noted above, it should be evident that they proceeded differently. The emotional reactions to the cause are different, the seriousness of the event is underscored by legal prosecution possibilities in the second case, and the historical investment in relationships was more entrenched in the second case. When we take into account the reason for the dismissal and our relationship with the dismissed employee, we understand that each termination is a unique event. Realizing this uniqueness helps us as we prepare ourselves for the interview.

Preparing Yourself for the Interview

Once we have reached the point of no return (or so we think), it is time to assess our readiness to conduct the termination interview. The place to begin is with ourselves. This chapter asks us to devote time and energy willingly to the task of assessing our own strengths and weaknesses. This undertaking requires some soul-searching and a willingness to be honest with ourselves. Some of us find this honesty hard to come by as we attempt to examine what we bring to the termination interview. In the process of terminating it is always easier to blame the employee than to lay any responsibility on our own shoulders.

Surely few of us can admit that we have never made mistakes. Nor can we say that we have never talked with others about mistakes that they have made.

What are our own greatest fears about the termination itself? Are we concerned that we might lose control of the interview, that we might back down, that the other person will say or do something that catches us off guard—or that we simply won't know what to do? Generally, loss of control, loss of credibility, and loss of the words to convey our message are what we fear most in difficult situations. We can all think of times when our abilities to handle the sending and receiving of difficult messages has been tested. Perhaps—

- We have told someone we love that a close friend or relative has died.
- We have admitted making dangerous or costly mistakes.
- We regretfully explained why a birthday wish could not be granted.
- We informed a romantic partner that our needs were not being met.
- We prepared the stockholders for the bad news that revenues dropped 25% last quarter.
- We told our family that it was going to be uprooted because we had accepted a job halfway across the country that would mean more money and more challenging work.

Our experience is clearly more extensive than this partial list can indicate.

To increase our own ability to maintain control of the termination interview, consider those conditions that could hinder us from organizing and following through with our termination plans. We each have our own idiosyncratic ways of coping with the world. Just as surely there are weaknesses in this coping strategy. Certain types of statements make us angry, defensive, guilty, sad, disgusted, or resentful. It is better to discover the sorts of statements that can produce these feelings in us and neutralize them before we hear them in the termination interview. What we hear in the interview can attack us where we are most vulnerable. Responses from terminees may be any of the following:

1. "You're not fair!"
2. "You don't care about me."
3. "I always knew you would treat me this way."
4. "How am I supposed to feed my family?"
5. "Other people get away with murder. You are picking on me!"
6. "I know where you live—boy, are you gonna pay!"

 7. "I didn't mean to do it."

 8. "You never told me what you wanted."

 9. "You set me up."

10. "You're right. I have not been working very hard, but I know I can change. Give me a chance."

11. "You know I've had a lot of family problems, of course I have been affected by that. I'll come through for you."

12. "I don't know what I am going to do now."

13. Sobbing.

14. "Okay. Now that I know what you think of me, let me tell you what I think of you. You're a narrow-minded, nosey boss who only cares what the guys upstairs are going to say."

15. "Yeah, sure, you just don't like me. I knew that from the beginning."

Sample responses to these statements are given at the end of this chapter. Could you easily respond to any of them?

Our primary goal in the interview should be to process the message of termination with the employee. If we are distressed and in pain, angry, or irritable, it will be impossible to offer the employee the support he or she needs to understand and respond to the termination in the most appropriate way.

To gain familiarity with our own trouble spots and areas of vulnerability, follow this procedure. Think back over the last year. Ask yourself what situations have caused you the most distress. List them on a sheet of paper. For example:

- "When my boss told me that a secretary had filed charges of sexual harassment against him."

- "When my wife told me she wanted to quit her job and go back to school."

- "When the bank told me that there was a legal judgment against me and refused to lend me money it had promised—only to find out it was someone else named Johnson who owed the money."

- "Waiting in line for an hour only to be told they are closing early for lunch."

After clearly identifying each situation, go back and honestly examine your first reaction to that event. Write down your reaction and briefly recall what you said. Begin to look for patterns in your own behavior. Maybe you tend to ververbalize and sputter when presented with unusual or troublesome information. Perhaps you become tongue-tied or you may bluster angrily. Whatever your reactions, pay attention to them. This process will allow you to establish your own most likely reactions to unsettling messages.

Now you are ready to develop strategies to moderate and thus control these difficult communication patterns of yours. Remember:

1. Identify your own pressure points and vulnerabilities by honestly recalling your own behavior in other tense and difficult situations.

2. Recognize that many of the things said by the employee being terminated are said out of frustration and anger, not as considered opinions. The injured person often finds it consoling to know that the other will suffer as well.

3. It is your responsibility to maintain an even temper during the interview. Composure and assertiveness are your best defense against any sort of offense made by the employee. A cue to your own stress level is the quality and rhythm of your breathing. Keep it slow and constant. Using a modified biofeedback process, you can control your own anxiety.

4. Realize that you must keep the interview within the bounds of the issue at hand. Extraneous arguments should not be refuted by the manager. Generally you will disagree with the terminee's objections anyway; there is no need to add insult to injury.

5. At all costs prevent the interview from degenerating into a name-calling contest. It does not matter if the employee calls you an ogre. Let these symbols of anger go. Observe them, but do not let them get under your skin.

6. Treat each employee as a unique case. Avoid assuming that an approach that worked with one employee will work with another.

7. Practice role-playing a scene with a person you trust who will unload all of the "unfair" and "underhanded" comments that trip your anger or guilt. Develop reasonable responses to such charges.

8. Approach the interview as a learning experience. Gain as much information about your handling of the interview as possible.

9. Avoid discussion of the interview with anyone other than your immediate supervisors, trusted coworkers, or a special confidante. In the discussions of the interview, focus on objective information that you can clearly validate. Honestly assess your strengths and weaknesses.

10. Avoid any might-have-been's. Accept that the interview is over and that you did the best job you could, then move on to your

next task. Focusing unduly on the event forces it to take on more significance in your life than is helpful. Some managers carry memories of painful firings with them for years, making later terminations troublesome.

The more you are convinced that your actions were well motivated by concern for the company, your remaining staff, the employee in question, and your ability to perform your own job, the sooner you will be able to place the event in perspective.

When we are emotionally prepared, it is easier to confront the real issues ahead of us. Since we have reduced our ego-sensitivity toward the interview, we are now capable of objectively sensing the critical issues that will allow us to deliver the message and respond to the employee— however he or she chooses to deal with the situation. The employee may respond to our messages in a host of different ways, based on her/his maturity, emotional stability, and acceptance of change. To enhance our own capacities to function as we would like them to, we must organize the message with these guidelines for maintaining an objective and even emotional perspective in mind.

Organizing the Termination Message

With the worksheet in hand from Chapter Two, describing all of the key issues to be considered in the termination, we can plan our overall approach to the termination. In each interview, we should strive to introduce the issue straightforwardly, clarify the nature of the claims warranting termination, monitor the employee's reaction, identify departure procedures, explain severance packages where appropriate, and conclude the interview diplomatically.

Introducing the Issue Straightforwardly

Once all of the preparation for the interview is completed, we must call the person into a private office area and ask the person to be seated. If the person remains standing, it creates a difficult interaction style and may promote defensiveness. Idle chatter about the person's family, sports events, and other trivial data should be avoided. Introducing the issue often presents problems for managers who do not know where to begin. Those who have learned how to terminate over the years suggest (1) beginning with calm acknowledgment of the employee's presence through a greeting, (2) keeping the tone of the interview serious, and (3) briefly and succinctly stating the purpose of the meeting. Some managers advocate putting the announcement of dismissal in writing for the employee to read in their presence. Others choose to verbally introduce the decision. "John, we have reached the point we discussed with you a month ago. I have decided that termination of your employment is in our best interest." This statement cannot be vague. As with the letter or the verbal announcement, the interview then proceeds to the clarification stage.

Clarifying the Nature of the Claims

Each of the charges necessitating termination must be clarified, reminding the employee of the documentation supporting the decision. Naming the specific issues and ensuring that the person understands them are two different considerations. In high-stress situations listeners may hear the words, but because they are still responding to the first statement about termination, they may not take in what we say after the initial announcement. Hospital employees working in terminal wards and volunteers for hospices have learned this principle well. The grieving family and the patient may require several tellings of the story.

Monitoring the Employee's Reaction

Identify which of the typical responses the person is experiencing. Some will accept the decision; others will want to refute the message. We must listen to the person's reaction, indicating that we have heard their statement. We are not compelled to disagree, merely to accept their reaction as legitimate for them. It is helpful to remember that when a person rejects our messages, they reject our messages, not necessarily us. Detachment is crucial for the manager at this point. We must avoid identifying so strongly with the employee's feelings that we are pulled into his or her own personal conflict. Statements like, "I see," or "would you mind explaining?" can be helpful if the person begins to make charges directed at us. Even saying, "I understand what you are saying," can encourage conversation about the firing without promoting acquiescence.

Identifying Departure Procedures

Just as performance appraisals clarify the expected goals, the termination interview should describe our expectations of the leave-taking process. This may include special loose ends that must be tied up; the person may need time to settle his or her affairs. However, terminees should never be expected to train their replacements. Most managers prefer to usher the person out of the workforce as quickly as possible, for their sake and to maintain employee morale. If outplacement services are part of our agreement with the employee, then the process may be slightly slower.

Explaining Severance Procedures

Exit benefits can ease the pain. The severance package may be substantial and relatively complicated if it is based on profit-sharing plans and the like. Because of the complexity, a personnel representative should clarify these issues, but they should be introduced by you. When possible, our willingness to write letters of recommendation can help to stabilize the employees. A relatively common practice is to suggest to the employees that while you do not feel you could recommend them for another job at the same level, you would be happy to verify the employment dates upon request.

Concluding the Interview Diplomatically

The closing comments of the dismissal interview can be as important as the opening ones. It is these words that the employee takes with him or her to the exit. In a termination interview, the conclusion is not a typical closing. In most leave takings we make promises to "see you around" or imply some future contact. This is an irregular event in termination and one that should be guarded against. Natural sentiments that demonstrate concern may have a boomerang effect with some dismissed employees. "Best of luck!" may be appropriate for someone we have talked through all the issues with and who accepts the decision as best. Addressed to the passive-aggressive person, such words could instigate a blow-up because they can be interpreted as a sign of insincerity.

Phrases that signal conclusion are important as they release us and the terminee from a troublesome event. Some sample phrases note the winding down of the interview: "Personnel will be expecting you in a few minutes. I think we have discussed everything we need to discuss." While we may honestly feel like saying, "I'm so sorry," it is often best to refrain from making statements like this because the natural response from the employee is, "If you felt so bad, why did you let me go?" Avoid making promises of assistance to the employee if they are not realistic.

When the Employee Stays on Past the Termination

If for some reason the employee must stay on for two weeks or more after having been terminated several important issues must be considered. The person who is separated should not be expected to function in meetings with those who will continue on in their jobs. Communication with the person will take on a different tone, one that is more formal, less personal. Casual inquiries about the subordinate from the manager who has terminated—like, "What are your Christmas plans?"—should be avoided as they assume that the questioner has a right to an answer. The truth of the matter is that with the dismissal and message of rejection, the manager loses all right to access the other person's private plans.

A final reminder: during this time and immediately preceding the termination, we cannot afford to denigrate or in any way take advantage of the person. Employees to be terminated or who have been terminated should never be asked to interview others for jobs. They should be separated from interviewing candidates for their own position as much as possible. These actions only create more resentment than necessary and fuel some employees' desires for revenge.

Employee Reactions to Dismissal

Some of the most common reactions to being fired are: (1) anticipation of the event, (2) disbelief or shock, (3) escape or flight, (4) euphoria, (5) violence, (6) depression, (7) emotional outbursts like crying, and (8) positive behavior such as assuming responsibility for the situation. These reactions are accompanied by a variety of emotions, including anger, shame, fear, sadness, self-pity, or courage. Each of these reactions requires a clear and reasonable response to stabilize the interview.

Anticipation of the Event (Acceptance)

One of the easier reactions to cope with occurs when the employee knows the axe will fall. He or she has probably already made other plans, realizing that the present situation is not going to improve. In such instances you will find little resistance to your plan of delivering the message in the most rational environment possible. Managers have indicated in significant numbers that termination interviews in which the employee agreed are the easiest interviews and the least defensive (Michal-Johnson, 1981).

Disbelief or Shock

Disorientation is the key to a response of disbelief, whether it is registered in a belligerent or passive way. The employee has either deluded himself or herself that the situation is improving or has found a variety of ways to explain it away. Because the person is convinced it will work out, the dismissal serves to unsettle his/her mental processes and emotional stability. The person who cannot believe that termination is occurring is one to take care with. It is perfectly understandable for people essentially to have the wind knocked out of them after the message has been stated. In this situation we must calmly restate the decision. The disoriented person will literally find it difficult to accept that he or she has heard us correctly. At first, repeating the message can be very important. With a person who proclaims, "I can't believe you are firing me!," take care to restate the case. For instance, "You know, John, we have talked about this issue on three separate occasions. There is no alternative in this case. We have attempted to find ways to work out the problem—all to no avail. I'm afraid the decision is final. I can assure you that I have carefully evaluated your case. I ask that you review the performance goals we established on March 1. The goals clearly indicate that the production reports will be in my office no later than two days after the information reaches your desk. Since that time your reports have consistently been three or four days past this deadline. I have no choice." After such a response, we will want to clarify the terms of the termination, including when it is effective, how we want the person to vacate the work place, what specific benefits we have made available, and what resources we are willing to commit to the person for job search.

Escape or Flight

Not at all unlike the fight-or-flight response typical of animals under siege, the escape reaction indicates the individual's difficulty in coping with the moment. He or she is likely to agree hastily in order to leave the scene. Such a premature exit can short-circuit a more productive acceptance on the part of the employee. Normal conversation is side-stepped and the interview can be tense because of the clear desire of the employee to leave.

To say this response is unhealthy may be going too far. In talking with the employee who wants to flee, the manager first has to recognize the condition. Attempting to hurry the message, nonresponsiveness, or constant looking at the exit can cue the manager that the employee has an urge to run away from the event. While we can hardly restrain a person so inclined, it is reasonable for us to attempt to engage him or her in conversation. Say, for example, "we want to validate your understanding" or "Make sure you understand the arrangements to be made. We want to explain the severance plan; please ask questions if you have them." If we cannot detain the person, we can send him or her to a personnel representative trained in exit interviewing or counseling in order to process the experience.

Delight

Some employees may appear to be delighted by their dismissal. Although this may sound implausible, it does happen. Employees who respond this way may be expressing their relief that a decision has finally been made. Still others may seem delighted because they are people pleasers and do not want to appear ungrateful. If such a defense mechanism is operating, the employee is sabotaging his or her own legitimate reaction of anger or dismay. Approaching the delighted terminee requires some skill in encouraging the person to examine his or her true feelings about the event. The person might be addressed as follows. "You are certainly taking this very well. In fact I am surprised that you are not feeling a little disappointed. I know I certainly would be if I were in your shoes."

Violence

Though violence is not common, it is a reaction we must anticipate. Many organizations routinely have the security force supervising the employee who might become angry and physically abusive. Before terminating someone, determine whether that person could easily overpower you or has a belligerent nature. In any event, ensure that you have a witness. If the cause of termination is in any way related to a legal infringement, security guards must be called in. In the event of the theft of narcotics from a pharmacy, malicious destruction of property, accusations of fighting with other employees, or the like—expect the worst.

Several strategies can aid in defusing a potentially violent situation. First, state calmly, "You must not lose control of yourself. Please sit down. I will listen to you." In cases where the employee is making enough noise to drown out a calm voice, repeat the previous direction in a firm and unyielding voice. You might also clarify that you do not want the person to suffer more than he is obviously suffering now. If verbal threats are followed by physical threats, engage the restraining support of security guards.

The anger felt by the employee must find an appropriate outlet. Frequently, angry people insinuate they will inflict harm to the manager or the company at some future date. Take this seriously and be cautious, realizing that the vast majority will not act on this impulse.

An angry person cannot be reasoned with. We must allow time for their feelings to subside. Most people, it should be noted, will still be functioning in a state of disbelief and will not be capable of immediate reprisals.

Why is it that some employees lose their sense of perspective and vent their anger in such unproductive and dangerous ways? There are clearly some deep-seated psychological stakes involved. Each of us has built up a concept of ourselves from infancy that has been modified by our interactions with others. Part of this self-concept is centered in acceptance by others whom we deem important to us. Because managers are in positions of authority, employees may look to us for support and validation of their self-concept. In the termination interview it seems clear to the employee that we no longer value his or her work. The interview can cause those with low self-esteem to experience a dramatic decline in their sense of self-worth, resulting in depression (internalized anger and helplessness) or externally directed anger. It is the latter sort of individual who seems more likely to engage in overt revenge actions.

To the disturbed employee, violent action appears to punish the employer, either for making a bad decision or for singling the employee out for "unfair" punishment. We may not be able to understand why some individuals act out their frustration in the extreme ways they do. It may help to recall for a moment how we have suffered when something we very much wanted was denied. We have all experienced rejection of one sort or another, and perhaps we can see extreme reactions are in proportion to the rejection felt by the dismissed employee. The more violent the reaction, the more violent the perceived attack on the self-esteem of the individual. Careful attention to the process of the interview can help avert some of the unfortunate outcomes.

Depression

The depressed employee is generally unable to become angry with others and so turns the anger inward. Depression may take the form of listlessness, disorientation, and assuming the posture of a victim. "If I had only" seems to dominate the reaction of such people. As with many of the other responses, the best strategy is to put yourself in the listening position. Ask the person to describe his or her own contribution to the company. You may tell them about aspects of their work life that are positive, so long as it is clear that these in no way negate the cause for termination. Talk about severance benefits or where they should go after leaving your office.

Crying

Our stereotypes may lead us to expect people who respond by crying to be female. It may surprise us to know that nearly as many men as women break down and cry. Crying is a more socially sanctioned response for women than men, but terminations jeopardize the family life style and challenge the masculine role as profoundly as they do the feminine role. Women who terminate men and observe them crying tend to want to make them stop. Crying is a legitimate way to display feelings and should not be cut short. Allow those who are overwhelmed by their feelings to cry it out. Give them time to get themselves together. Whatever you say, do not tell them, "There's nothing to cry about. You're still alive, aren't you?" Accept crying as a natural and normal response, perhaps even a desirable one.

Positive Behavior

If the employee has reached the decision that this job is not right for her or him, the act of termination is simply the other shoe dropping, an act of completion. Generally, positive behavior occurs when you have developed an effective working relationship with the person and she or he respects you and fully appreciates your position.

Whether or not the employee responds to the dismissal as you expected, the following guidelines should help you construct the message.

General Guidelines for Constructing Messages of Termination

Phrasing Statements

Use of pronouns When phrasing statements to the employee regarding performance, begin with "I" or "me" or "we" statements. "It is clear to *me* that *our* counselling about tardiness has not worked out. *I* am confused by your attitude. In the last counselling session *I* specifically recall that *we* agreed that after one more unauthorized tardiness it would be necessary for you to leave. As you can see, today you have come in late. We have no choice but to enforce the rules."

Ask "what" questions Never ask *why* an action was taken. This encourages more defensive posturing for the terminee. Instead, focus on *what* happened. Why's invite story-telling and introduce many irrelevant issues into the termination interview. "What" statements, on the other hand, allow individuals to see how they are explaining their own behavior. "What" responses are also easier to keep on track than "why" responses.

When an employee begins to ask "why" questions of you, the result will be similar. Rephrase the employee's question to you as a "what" question. For example: "So, what are the specific issues we had to consider when coming to this decision to ask you to leave? We looked at . . ."

Describing the Cause for Dismissal

Stick to the facts Objective information is easier to handle than subjective information. Keep any of your own explanations of the employee's behavior to yourself. Avoid statements like, "You obviously do not understand how this process works, nor will you ever learn." This is your frustration talking. Say instead, "We have discussed your failure to follow company procedures on filing expense reports repeatedly over the last six months."

Focus on the problem, not the person   "These actions are simply impossible for us to accept. We have had *three complaints* since our last discussion from customers who maintain that you promised them the tools in two weeks. Our turn-around time has always been three to four weeks. This practice has caused us to lose valuable customers. We can no longer afford to keep you on."

Responding to the Employee

Listen to the employee   The best way to ensure that you will listen is to stop talking. After you have made your point, allow the terminees to talk about the action, how they feel, and what they are going to do. Listening implies direct eye contact that is not judging but attentive. Make statements like, "Do you have any further questions about the severance package we are offering you?"

Accept threats without argument   If the employee threatens to sue you or your company, do not protest. Simply state, "That is certainly within your rights." You have nothing to worry about if you have documented and acted judiciously in the appraisal process.

Guide the interview   Keep the interview on track. If the employee strays and begins to introduce factors (for example the performance of others), use tracking statements like, "We really must not be concerned about the performance of others; my concern is your performance," or "The important thing for us both is to focus on the next few moments, not dwell on the past." By keeping the focus or ground of the interview in the present, not the past, you assist the employee to accept the decision.

Admitting When Help Is Needed

Keep your supervisor informed of the actions taken and the possibilities of reprisal. If you do not feel comfortable terminating the person by yourself, ask for help. Most supervisors will be happier to participate in the interview than to deal with any unpleasant aftermath. You can learn a great deal by observing.

The guidelines and suggestions in this chapter point clearly to one truth. Interviewing to dismiss is easier said than done. We must cope not only with the possible reactions of others, but our own vulnerabilities. To be in control of the interview, we can prepare ourselves for any eventuality that may be determined by the reason for the dismissal, the employee's reaction, or the nature of our relationship with the employee.

To assist in thinking about how we will actually address the dismissal, some sample situations and instructions for role-playing them are included in the Activity that concludes this chapter. You may want to ask the person who conducts training in your organization to assist you in developing helpful strategies for approaching each of these dismissal cases. Special instructions for the trainer or human resource expert who may be helping you are included immediately after the six cases reported in this section. It may be most helpful if you role-play the case that most closely resembles a situation you are currently facing.

SUMMARY

This chapter has served as basic training for those of us who will soon engage in dismissals. We must prepare ourselves mentally so that we are confident we can maintain control of the interview and minimize our own vulnerability. In addition, we can give some thought to likely scenarios that would prepare us for a host of possible employee reactions to the dismissal. We can also better cope with dismissals when we understand that the cause of dismissal and our relationship with the employee affects the likely response. Finally, a plan of action for conducting the interview must be developed, to ensure that we have approached the interview in the most humane and responsible way possible.

ACTIVITY: TRAINING YOURSELF FOR THE TERMINATION INTERVIEW

Many terminations occur just when you are not prepared for them. Ashleigh Brilliant's astute observation, "trouble always comes at the wrong time!" is as true as all of Murphy's laws. This module is geared to offer you the opportunity to think about your own skills and sharpen your own awareness of the termination interview and its aftermath. The cases mentioned below are taken from James Schreier's article in the *Training and Development Journal* of December 1980.

ASSESSING THE SITUATION

1. Read the description of the case you will be role-playing. From this description, identify the cause of termination, the documentation available, the presence of a thorough performance appraisal system, and the attitude of the manager toward termination.

2. Plan a strategy for presenting the termination message. Establish the tone you desire in the interview. Identify your opening statement, your description of the conditions of termination (cause) and prepare to respond appropriately to the terminee's reaction.

3. Another person should be selected to role-play the terminee in this trial interview. He or she will be given instructions about how to respond.

4. A third party has been asked to serve as a facilitator and observer of the actions of both parties' communication skills and effectiveness. If possible your interview will be videotaped to allow you to see how you handle problematic responses.

5. Process the interview with the observer. Identify those word choices that could produce difficulty. Monitor your own feelings and reactions in the process. What was most difficult for you? What was easiest? How will the real situation differ from this role-played one? What can you do to account for those differences?

6. Go over the questions about the termination from Chapter Two regarding an employee of yours that you are currently having difficulty with. Write your own case study using the Stern case as a model. Identify the reactions you think are possible and teach the role-playing partner about the terminee. Plan the interview and videotape it with your observer on hand to assist you in gaining perspective on your own behavior.

7. Pay attention to (a) how well you handle criticism, (b) your willingness to accept the judgments of others without refuting and debating the issues, (c) your ability to alter your behavior based on reasonable feedback from others.

CASE STUDIES

Employee 1

Daniel Stern is a 26-year-old Manager of Promotion Services in the Aqua Ski Division. He was promoted to the position 12 months ago after two successful years as a member of the department's Promotional Ski Team. His current salary base is $16,000. He completed only three years of college (in athletic education), dropping out to join a ski show. His performance in the management position has never met expectations. Numerous conferences concerning his failure to meet performance standards, his difficulties in supervising his staff, and his frequent absences have failed to result in any improvements.

Recommendation of Division Manager: TERMINATION.

Employee 2

Joyce Sloan, 53, has spent 32 years with Tennis Dynamics in a variety of positions, varying from file clerk to her current position as Administrative Support Manager at an annual salary of $24,000. In the last five years, her performance has slipped significantly as she failed to keep up with technological improvements, particularly in word processing. Attempts to retrain her have been unsuccessful and she has refused reassignment to a lower position.

Recommendation of Administrative Vice President: TERMINATION.

Employee 3

Louis Torbert, 38, has been employed for eight years as a Staff Trainer in the Corporate Training Department. A former high school teacher, Torbert has consistently received above-average to excellent ratings on his training classes and his performance appraisals. His current salary, at $21,000, is slightly above some other staff trainers who have longer service records with the company. He is, however, the junior member of the department. The Corporate Personnel Department has ordered a 10% reduction in staff because of the declining economic conditions of the nation.

Recommendation from Director of Corporate Training: TERMINATION.

Employee 4

James Bart, 57, has been the Financial Vice-President of the company for twenty years and currently earns $38,000 annually. He came with the company when it was first incorporated and grew with it. He was an excellent performer until four or five years ago when the company began to expand rapidly through new markets and acquisitions. Now his performance is below average; in many ways, Bart is holding the company back through outdated financial management. Discussion and seminars have failed to have a significant impact. Junior financial managers are becoming frustrated (one quit) because he does not allow them to use newer techniques.

Recommendation from Executive Vice President: TERMINATION.

Employee 5

Kathleen Jordan, 32, has been a Supervisor in the Production Assembly Department for three years, earning $17,000. She was promoted from an assembly worker (after two years) as part of an equal opportunity training program. Now, the very program which gave her the opportunity to advance has resulted in consistently poor performance ratings. She is incapable of getting along with colleagues and subordinates. In the last 12 months numerous discrimination complaints have been filed against the company because of her practices. Only one has not been justified.

Recommendation of Assembly Department Manager: TERMINATION.

Employee 6

Dolores Hamilton, 46, is a Senior Product Designer and has been with the company in various design capacities for nineteen years. At $30,000 annually, her salary is below average for her pay range. Difficulties began several years ago with a slight decline in her design quality and the occasional comment that she wasn't keeping up with changes. The decline accelerated three years ago when her husband died suddenly. Her contributions to the department have been virtually none. She is currently being assigned to routine design modifications usually given to junior staff members.

Recommendation of Product Design Manager: TERMINATION.

ROLE PLAY INSTRUCTIONS

You have been assigned one of the roles representing the characters involved in this exercise. Read carefully the background information and the description of your character. Prepare to "become" this character by studying the data on age, experience, background, and salary. Your responses should be appropriate to the character and the guidelines presented below.

Caution: In some roles you are aware of the impending termination, in others you are "suspicious," and in others you are totally unaware. Study your characterization carefully.

Response: Daniel Stern

Your reaction to your termination is simply shock and disbelief. "How could you possibly do this to me?" This can't be happening—everything has been going well. Your reaction may or may not include acknowledging any previous discussions concerning the situation.

Response: Joyce Sloan

Your reaction to your termination is rage and anger—anger at your boss, fellow employees, other supervisors, and the company itself. You are going to do little that is constructive except blow off steam and blame it on the other guy. There is very little chance that you are willing to discuss job performance—unless your boss does an excellent job of relieving your anger and changing your focus.

Response: Louis Torbert

Your reaction to your termination is a complicated psychological process generally called a defense mechanism. Specifically your reaction may be one of several; pick one that you can play well. *Escape* or *avoidance* involves fleeing from the situation or refusing to talk or think about it. *Denial* involves a complete rejection of the reality, including continuing to work, not telling family and friends.

Response: James Bart

Your reaction to your termination is one of distress, depression, and/or despair. The situation to you is hopeless and this extends beyond the job situation—your entire life is hopeless. Outside the job this could extend to loss of appetite, insomnia, etc.

Response: Kathleen Jordan

Your reaction to your termination is reflective grief. If only you had acted differently, if only you had done this instead of that, if only you had taken a different course of action, things would have been different. Talk consistently about things in the past and how they could be different.

Response: Dolores Hamilton

Your reaction to your termination is positive behavior that reflects a desire to get on with life. You acknowledge the termination and start immediately to express concern about your strengths, weaknesses, and interests. You're eager to find out about job hunting skills, references, and other things that will get you out and looking immediately.

USING THE CASE STUDIES FOR TRAINING AND DEVELOPMENT

The cases above will allow you, the human resource developer, to work with managers and direct their understanding of the termination process.

Resources

You will need a videotape system to record and play back the termination interviews that will be role-played.

You must be willing to serve as an observer or facilitator for the processing, of the role plays or draw in someone else who is trained in these skills. Processing includes asking questions of the manager regarding intent, examining specific communication strategies and their effectiveness, and assessing the ability of managers to follow through on planned strategies and to deviate when a strategy is no longer working.

Locate a person who can comfortably take on a variety of roles and will accept the assignment seriously.

One of the liabilities of this process is that it requires enactment or recreation. You must do everything humanly possible to make the simulation adhere as closely as possible to the real situation. This means you will have to train an individual to take on the roles listed in this series of cases. There are six roles and six different reactions mandated. You must take them seriously.

Process

You may want to work with managers individually or in groups. This will depend on the sensitivity of the manager to feedback from others and the maturity of the managers. The best results and change occur in working with groups, but consider what is appropriate in your situation.

Each manager will role-play one of the cases and then role-play a real situation that they are currently considering for termination.

Follow the questions on the manager's sheet to determine your role in processing these role plays.

SAMPLE RESPONSES TO DIFFICULT EMPLOYEE REACTIONS

Earlier in this chapter we listed fifteen different employee reactions to the message of dismissal. In the following section, you will find some sample responses to these difficult reactions. Do not limit yourself to the examples provided. Ask yourself, "How would I most likely respond to this sort of statement?"

1. "You're not fair."

"I'm sorry you feel that way. I want to go over with you the performance appraisals of the last several months and clarify the opportunities you have had to change your performance.

2. "You don't care!"

    "Caring for you is not the issue right now. I do care that we handle this interview appropriately."

3. "I always knew you would treat me this way."

    "I'm sorry you feel that I have always wanted to hurt you. I can tell you now that I have never been aware of wanting to hurt you. Of course this decision is a difficult one to adjust to."

4. "How am I supposed to feed my family?"

    "Feeding your family is certainly a problem. You will be able to support them. There are a number of people you can turn to."

5. "Other people get away with murder. You are picking on me."

    "We all function within the same rules. This conversation has nothing to do with others, but has everything to do with your performance."

6. "I know where you live—boy, are you gonna pay."

    "Threatening me will not give you your job back. I really do not want to see you get into any more trouble."

7. "I didn't mean to do it!"

    "I'm sure you never intended to do it, but the fact is, it was done. We cannot change that or take it back, even though both of us might like to. We must go on from here."

8. "You never told me what you wanted!"

    "Let's examine these performance appraisal statements about your goals for the last two months. They should help clarify this concern of yours."

9. "You set me up."

    "I'm sorry you feel that way. We have talked about these issues on several occasions. You said you understood they would have to change."

10. "You're right. I have not been working very hard, but I know I can change. Give me a chance."

    "I'm afraid that's a luxury we cannot afford. There have been chances in the past. There are no more chances here."

11. "You know I have had family problems, of course I have been affected by them. I'll come through for you."

    "I know you have had problems and in the past we have given you time to adjust and take care of those problems. We have carried you as long as we could hoping that the situation would change. It simply has not changed."

12. "I don't know what I'm going to do now."

    "Once you have had time to sort all of this out, you will find what's best for you to do. Talk with our personnel representative, who is skilled in this area."

13. Sobbing

    Allow the person to cry. Don't tell them to stop—it is a way of releasing frustration.

14. "O.K. Now that I know what you think of me, let me tell you what I think of you."

    "I don't want us to leave on this note. I know you are angry. I'd like to tell you what the company can offer you to assist you financially for the next few weeks.

15. "Yeah, sure, you don't like me."

    "We're talking about your job performance now."

_____

4

AFTER THE INTERVIEW: WHAT NOW?

We may feel that once the dismissal has occurred, our obligations are over. This, however, is not the case. The change has been put into motion, but the ripples of the action will begin to affect everyone involved in short order. Managers can learn a lot from processing the interview and placing it in perspective, just as the terminated employee can as he or she attempts to put the pieces back together.

Managers: What Is There to Learn?

Each person conducting a termination interview has an opportunity in the few hours immediately following the interview to evaluate his or her conduct of the dismissal. First, we can review the cautions we have observed (see the checklist at the end of Chapter Two). Second, we can ask ourselves questions about the interview, as though we were experiencing a post-interview debriefing.

- Which cautions were most difficult to implement?
- Did we respond to difficult reactions in an effective way?
- Were we able to maintain a sense of calm in the interview? Was our breathing slow and normal or did our pulse race out of control?
- Did we follow the plan developed for the interview? If not, where did we deviate? Was the alteration a sign of flexibility or loss of control?
- Did the employee respond as expected? If not, what behavior was surprising?
- Was the issue of termination confronted, rather than the person being terminated?
- Was the interview kept on track by asking questions and responding in ways that minimized tangents?
- Were statements made that perhaps should not have been? What were they?

Monitoring the Interview

To ensure that we are able to benefit from the experience of termination and apply our understanding of it to other situations that will inevitably follow, we should begin a file on the terminations we have conducted. This file can be kept in a locked file cabinet to ensure security and confidentiality. It should be written by each manager, not by the manager's secretary. The file will function as a survival kit, but only for the manager who prepares it. The file should contain general biographical information such as the position, length of service, cause for termination, and the terms of settlement. Names are not necessary. Take about thirty minutes to replay the interview in your mind. Treat the event as a Hollywood script writer might. Recreate in your own words what happened in this termination, the more detail the better. Go through the script and edit for accuracy. Star those aspects of the termination that were easier. Put an X by those that were more difficult.

Now, give yourself a grade. If you could give yourself such a mark, which would it be?

A = Superior

B = Good

C = Average

D = Poor

F = Failing

Look over the scenario again and identify the positive actions taken. What were your strengths in counseling, evaluating, and disciplining the specific person? Now, identify the negative actions. What might be considered weaknesses in the negative approach?

Breaking the News to the Work Group

While the specific conditions of the termination are confidential and constitute a trust between manager and former employee, the issue must be addressed honestly and carefully for those who remain. Sample statements which may be used to clarify the situation are listed below.

(*Opening*) "I know that you are concerned that _____ is no longer with us. I wanted to assure you that we will continue to keep this department moving."

(*Opening*) "The events of the last few days have been difficult ones. I want you to understand that _____'s leaving will affect us all for a while, but that all of us will adjust to it in time."

(*Issue disclosure*) "You may be concerned about _____'s departure. It is our policy to ensure that discussions with employees who are leaving remain confidential. We hope that you can appreciate this decision. This is essentially a very private matter."

(*Addressing the fears of employees*) "This action cannot be interpreted as cause for concern for your own positions. There is no need to worry about your own tenure here with us."

(*Closing*) "If you have a specific difficulty that _____'s leaving will create, please talk with me about it as soon as possible. We will try to take care of any problems that might arise. Let's get back to our own jobs now."

These sample statements are intended merely to give direction. Each manager will tailor the message to meet his or her own natural style. Sincerity in delivering the messages is of prime importance. If we make statements that are not genuine for us, our employees will see through the masquerade.

The goal of such statements is to stabilize the remaining workforce by slowing down the rumor mill and assuring those who continue that they have no reason for concern. If there will be additional cutbacks in the near future, this needs to be addressed honestly. False promises at this point can boomerang dangerously on the organization.

Most employees will see the writing on the wall if the dismissed employee has been terminated for job incompetence, interpersonal incompetence, or a rule violation. In general, there is little sympathy for the dismissed employee unless employees feel the action was not justified. Employees who continue are more likely to avoid the person because he or she is no longer "one of us." When the daily contact of coworkers with the terminee is either diminished or severed, the coworkers can shift their focus from the termination event back to work. Because the person is not present to remind them of the issues and the event, they can shift attention to rebuilding the work team.

One thing to keep in mind in announcing the terminee's departure is the need for confidentiality. Employees who remain must be reassured that should they be terminated, their circumstances will not be paraded before others. Communicating carefully at this juncture helps to preserve the employee's dignity.

In the hours and days immediately following the dismissal of a worker, managers must keep the office functioning. During this period we must process the event ourselves and assist others in adjusting to the decision. As managers, we can learn from reviewing the separation interview, planning the separation announcement to the staff, and reassuring those who remain.

The Employee's Side: Assisting the Dismissed Employee

As we go back to our jobs, dealing with the next crisis at hand, the employee departs to a world that is not the same as it was before. The change has not registered completely. Can the person comfortably go back to the desk, the truck, or the lounge? Is it suddenly foreign territory? Morin and Cabrera (1982), outplacement consultants for Drake, Beam and Morin, have suggested that the next seventy-two hours are crucial for the departing employee. The attitude carried through the three days following termination can be seen as an indicator of the psychological health and adjustment potential of the terminee. How can we assist employees confronted with this crisis? First, simply understanding what the person will experience can broaden our perspective on the entire spectrum of termination events. Second, such an understanding can motivate us to assist our organization in offering a variety of assistance options to the dismissed employee.

What Often Happens?

Anyone confronted with a message of rejection (and dismissal is rejection) faces a period of reorientation. The upheaval resulting from dismissal generates confusion of identity and questions the person's capacity to cope. The person who has been terminated functions in a state of emotional and informational overload. It is easy to view this event as a personal catastrophe. Moreover, it is an action that directly affects the individual's family members as well as those encountered in his or her public life. The extent of the rippling effects of termination is determined by the willingness of the employee to readjust perceptions and redirect his or her energies. Each of these factors should be considered as we evaluate the employee's "coping quotient."

Attitudes First, we can all expect that we might feel rotten if we were fired. Within this framework, though, a host of conflicting perceptions and attitudes might plague us. We might feel guilty for making mistakes, ashamed of our transgressions, hopeless that we will ever have another job, and angry at our own sense of failure. These reactions erode the confidence and self-esteem that workers must have in order to function successfully. To reduce the burden of these negative attitudes and redirect energy toward more positive outcomes, the dismissed employee must be encouraged to view this as a new beginning, not as an end. Beginnings require action.

It is difficult to acquire this healthy rebounding attitude. Countless individuals choose to buy into the negative aspects of termination and thus make the experience significantly worse than it need be. Edward is typical of this reaction. A fifty-five-year-old airplane industry employee, laid off a year ago, he is still looking for work. He lives in constant hope that he will be recalled. His job-hunting is half-hearted. He has moved out of state, spends most of his days watching television, complains about how hard it is to get a job, and makes no progress toward employment.

He waits passively for someone out there to push the magic button that will give him his job back. In the interim, his attitude has deteriorated. People do not enjoy being around him because he has nothing positive to say and as the days pass he is farther and farther from his employment goal. Part of Edward's problem is his attitude. He views himself as a victim of circumstances and sees no alternatives to his present situation. Because his armed forces pension gives him enough to get by on, he traps himself in a rut of inaction. Edward has convinced himself that he is an economic pawn, that his life is in someone else's control. Edward is not unusual; many terminees have this same sort of immobilizing reaction. People without jobs must be able to create their own senses of hope. In the higher corporate echelons there may be more support in creating this hopefulness. For blue-collar workers with limited skills, it may become more frustrating because support systems are not so well developed for them as for management employees.

The irony of this dilemma is that when individuals are overwhelmed by a lack of hope and positive purpose, their chances of landing a good job are severely diminished. Employers will be hesitant to hire someone who is not in a position to sell himself or herself well. Because we carry our attitudes with us in our body language and our tone of voice, prospective employers can sense desperation and lack of confidence. To engage ourselves in the job-seeking process we must be mentally equipped with attitudes that will serve us well.

Some terminees will be able to redirect their lives without help, but many more require external motivators to set the job-finding process in motion. Closely related to the attitudes an individual displays upon termination is the emotional reaction to loss. Finley and Lee (1981) have talked about firing as a sort of death, with the same stages of emotional upheaval. They suggest that dismissed employees need help placing the termination event in perspective, seeking and receiving support and assistance, and resuming productive strategies. Figure 4-1 clearly sets forth these stages in Finley and Lee's model of readjustment.

Anyone who has experienced involuntary job separation will have a hard time placing the event in perspective immediately. Before sense can be made of the occurrence, Morin and Cabrera (1982) recommend that the person be allowed to ventilate his or her emotional reactions to the dismissal. Having the opportunity to release these feelings is an important step in the recovery process. When the emotions are bottled up and swallowed, more serious problems surface for the person later on. Ways to facilitate ventilation are discussed below in the description of the counseling interviews.

As mentioned earlier, people often respond to dismissal as they do to deaths of close relatives. Initially, the person may experience any of the four stages of death and dying as analyzed by Elizabeth Kübler-Ross (see

Figure 4-1

A Model of Outplacement Services for Terminated Executives, Detailing the States the Executive Goes Through and Counseling Strategies to Meet Each Need (Finley and Lee, 1981)

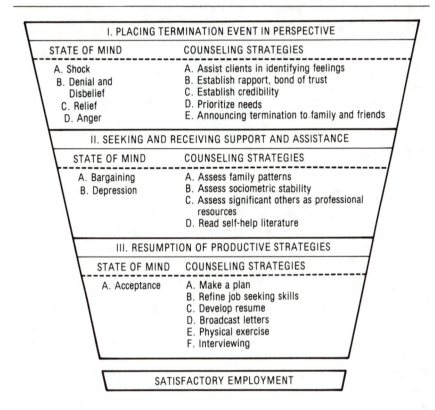

Figure 4-1). During this ventilation period the distressed individual may progress through shock, denial, disbelief, relief, and anger. Having an unbiased listener who can facilitate this first stage of adjustment may help relieve the terminee of excess emotional baggage. When individuals fail to experience these stages, they fail to mature in the experience and sabotage their futures. Kravetz (1978) tells of a man who refused to tell his family and friends of his dismissal and who maintained a charade of going to work every morning for an entire year. When his severance money ran out, he could no longer maintain the fiction.

The second stage of the terminee's grieving may include bargaining and depression. In the bargaining step the person attempts to strike deals with himself or herself, God, or the former boss, pleading that "If I can have my job back, I'll be good." When such bargaining does not work, depression often results. Anger with the situation turns inward and forces withdrawal. It is not until the individual is able to accept the action that reorientation can occur. An attitude of acceptance means that rebuilding can begin on firmer ground. Attempts to rebuild the person's career may falter until he or she comes to terms with the action of termination and puts it in the past. Suggestions for assisting employees through these stages are offered later in this chapter.

If we agree that the dismissal process for the terminated employee can be compared to the loss experienced through death, then the counseling strategies of loss are also likely to be comparable. In Figure 4-1, Finley and Lee (1981) have identified the counseling approaches most helpful in addressing each of the grieving stages cited in the left-hand column. It should be clear that the model applies to a long-term counseling effort; it would be inappropriate if applied to the exit interviewing process.

Support systems   The terminated employee may experience the separation traumas mentioned earlier, but he or she does not suffer them alone. The family and friends of the dismissed employee find themselves quickly involved in the process. Husbands and wives, children, parents, and neighbors are all people the terminee may turn to for support. While the person who has lost a job is going through turmoil, so is the person's family.

A management consulting firm specializing in outplacement counseling recently publicized a spouse counseling program developed to assist the spouse in adjusting to the termination. Frequently husbands and wives have built expectations of their mate that center on what it is that he or she does for a living. When these expectations are altered, often the relationship undergoes a change. Frequently, the spouse experiences as much disorientation as the separated employee. Changes that affect one will undoubtedly affect the other. Termination creates a situation requiring all parties in the family to pull together for mutual support. When the relationship was in trouble before the termination, the strain added to an already overloaded liaison can sometimes precipitate the dissolution of the marriage.

How family members respond to the news of dismissal also affects how the individual who is terminated views himself or herself. If the family rallies around the terminee, adjustment will be easier. However, if the firing is used to confirm preexisting questions about the competence and integrity of the person who has been dismissed, bad situations may become noticeably worse. For instance, when children are asked, "What does your father do?," they may be embarrassed that they cannot simply say, "He works for company X." Just as revealing the termination is difficult for the terminee, it is also difficult for family members.

The same may be true for friends and other associates. It is amazing to discover how much of our time in conversation relates to "the job." Even in the bowling league or the church study group, talk generally gets around to comments about work. The person who has been terminated suddenly finds that he or she cannot easily participate in such discussions. The awkwardness present in these interactions is largely due to the person's feelings of being a "have-not." Friends and associates may find that they are unwittingly contributing to this sense of awkwardness. This may be especially true in situations of introduction. Take the case in which a friend introduces the terminee to another and in conversation refers to the firm where the terminee used to work. The new party usually asks, "What are you doing now?" This usually harmless question is painful for the terminee and uncomfortable for the friend. In casual conversation and normal everyday circumstances, terminations become obvious and awkward obstacles to social interaction. By and large, there is little that can be done for the families and friends of terminees. The only way to assist these groups is to encourage the former employee to cope effectively with the situation.

Flexibility   A third factor contributing to the former employee's ability to turn the situation around is the natural resilience and flexibility of the individual. People who have narrowly defined themselves, who are unwilling to experiment, will find the adjustment to termination and reemployment more difficult than their counterparts who can see past the inconvenience of the moment. The person who is willing to try new and different jobs, to retrain, will fare better in the long run. Cultivating this experimental perspective can help those whose identities have been threatened by a dismissal. Closely related is the capacity to reach out and ask for help.

Finding a new job is a twenty-four-hour-a-day job. It will be affected by the attitudes terminees carry with them, the support their friends and families are able to offer, and their mental flexibility. If we are truly concerned about the adjustment of employees to the termination, there are several ways we can offer support. Post-termination counseling and career counseling, offered either by the company or outside agents, can help to stop the adjustment gap.

Posttermination Counseling

At least two different types of posttermination counseling are available to some terminees. One type, commonly referred to as exit interviewing, may have limited utility for the individual and the company. The other type, encouraging emotional discharge, may accomplish the greatest good for employees who have been terminated. It will be important to clarify the goals and possibilities of each counseling strategy, then compare and contrast each based on specific organizational needs.

Corporations may wish to study both voluntary and involuntary turnover in their organizations. A common research tool used to investigate turnover is the exit interview. In general, these exit interviews are conducted by personnel staff members, never by the manager who has terminated. Exit interviews can serve two functions, as noted by Downs, Smeyak, and Martin (1980): (1) to process the removal of the employee in an orderly way and (2) to collect information on the employee's reasons for leaving. The exit interview may thus serve to clarify severance pay, insurance premiums, pensions, and personal references as well as other topics, based on the circumstances. The second purpose, delving into the reasons for leaving, is usually more difficult to accomplish. While managers have already cited their official reasons for dismissal, it is helpful to give employees an opportunity to reveal their own views about why they have been terminated. In some cases the perceived reasons for termination differ radically.

Some advocates of exit interviews say that involuntary dismissals can be explored with employees, provided the interviewer is skilled in the process. Garrison and Ferguson (1977) suggest that the interviewer ask the employee what he or she perceives as the real cause for dismissal. Employees often believe their termination is for reasons other than those officially stated. It is sometimes possible in such interviews for personnel counselors to spot cases of wrongful dismissal, thereby averting a major fiasco. While employees who have just been terminated may not be able to articulate their own defenses in the termination interview with the manager, they may be able to do so with a third party. The interviewer is encouraged to refrain from either condemning or condoning any single action on the employee's part; instead, the interviewer should express empathy and understanding of the employee's perception of the dismissal event.

In the exit interview the counselor can also clarify rights of appeal and relevant procedures, should the employee feel that the termination violates company policies or procedures. If union representation is important, it may be advisable to have the shop steward attend the interview as well. Should arbitration be an alternative, then the process can be explained fully.

As typically conducted, the exit interview is not a realistic opportunity for ventilating a terminee's pent-up feelings about the dismissal. It is likely to be systematic and geared toward clarifying information. While soon-to-be ex-employees are reeling from the news of termination, their information processing skills are at a minimum distorted by their emotional reactions to the event.

An alternative approach, specifically designed for dismissed individuals, is advocated by Kravetz (1978). He sees the primary goal of such an interview, conducted by a highly skilled counselor with psychological training, as helping to steer the terminee away from possible negative overreaction and distortion. Morin and Cabrera (1982) consider the counselor's role a vital part of the outplacement process, as well. From their perspective, the counselor must be capable of:

- Building a rapid rapport with the client.
- Promising and maintaining absolute confidentiality with the client. (If unethical or inappropriate reasons have been used by the manager, or the manager's behavior is questioned, the counselor may seek to notify the manager's supervisor to ensure that such actions will not be repeated.)
- Giving the person undivided positive attention.
- Counseling, including listening, probing, and observing.
- Referring the person to appropriate support services.
- Ensuring that benefits and procedures have been addressed.

The counseling interview to facilitate emotional adjustment can serve as a buffer between the termination interview and re-entry into the outside world. It can be used to defuse overreactions by the employee. However, it should be noted that individuals conducting such counseling sessions must be carefully trained as counselors. Unskilled individuals asked to perform such delicate interviews can exacerbate the problem, thus unintentionally encouraging the terminee to act out extreme behaviors.

Kravetz (1978) reiterates the importance of establishing clear goals and standards of performance by managers as a way of reducing the shock of dismissal for job incompetence. The shocked response can occur, however, even when the employee seems to understand the criteria for evaluation.

In such cases it is the counselor's job to help the terminee voice feelings of shock, anger, disbelief, or acceptance. Skilled counselors interviewing dismissed employees will probe into how the person is feeling, rather than asking why he or she feels a particular way. Statements that give the client permission to voice feelings often suggest that certain types of reactions are normal. For example, "situations like this often make us angry; what is it about this action that makes you the angriest?"

When the counselor is employed by the company, it may be difficult to convince the dismissed employee of the counselor's sincerity. It is normal for the exiting employee to question the motives of the counselor. The terminee is likely to feel that the counselor is an arm of the former boss; that information shared will not be confidential and will harm future job applications. Morin and Yorks (1982) cite the example of an employee who felt that the company's counselor would track him into jobs where he would not work for the company's competition. The counselors were able to indicate that a number of employees who had left the firm were presently working for the competition. Once the barriers between the in-house counselor and the client are broken down, the counselor can help the individual establish viable career goals and create a reasonable job search plan. Although it may be desirable to establish a counseling link with the terminee that eases their reentry, companies should encourage the terminee to establish a support system outside the company that can offer long-term assistance.

The two types of posttermination interviews discussed in this section differ dramatically. Traditional exit interviews function to increase company information about benefits, final paycheck, severance benefits and to encourage evaluation of company operations. In some instances they attempt to clarify the individual's perception of why the dismissal occurred. The counseling interview, on the other hand, presumes that a process like the exit interview has already occurred; it allows the individual to begin the process of ventilating his/her emotional reactions to termination. The person skilled in exit interviewing might not always be prepared for the more therapeutic interview discussed by Kravetz (1978).

A more comprehensive program which includes therapeutic intervention is available through outplacement services. It is estimated that approximately 75 percent of the 1500 largest U.S. corporations use outplacement firms to assist terminated executives. While the counseling interview discussed earlier ceases to benefit the individual after the initial adjustment period, outplacement is designed to render the displaced employee employable.

Outplacement

Walking into the main offices of an outplacement firm in a prestigious Houston high-rise, past the heavy wooden doors, the oriental carpet, and the tasteful artwork, one has the sense that this is not a state employment commission office. The office trappings suggest opulence and financial success. The office serves managers, white-collar professionals, and executives with salaries ranging from $40,000 on up. Most outplacement firms cater to the elite ranks of the unemployed; factory workers and teachers will not find these organizations helpful.

One outplacement counselor who spoke with me described the program his firm has designed for "dehired" employees. First they provide ventilation counseling, diagnositc personality testing, and career development skills. The career development skills involve resumé preparation, interviewing training, marketing instruction, and negotiation guidelines.

Clients in this particular office were well-dressed businessmen in three-piece suits who had dressed for work. Each client is provided with secretarial support, desk space, telephones, and mailing privileges to assist them in their job search.

Given the cost of such services, it comes as no surprise that outplacement appears to be an expensive investment for the companies who use it. Generally, processing a former employee from dismissal to reemployment may take as long as five or six months, sometimes longer. The rule of thumb counselors use to calculate outplacement time is to plan a month of planning and search time for every $10,000 of the person's base salary. Thus a $50,000-a-year manager should expect to spend about five months in outplacement. The fees for these outplacement services range from 12 to 15 percent of the executive's base salary. While this may sound exorbitant, many companies find that in the long run it saves them money. When an employee's severance benefits are five, six, or even seven figures, the dollar savings can be substantial if the outplacement firm is able to assist the person in finding a replacement job in a relatively short period of time.

While outplacement works for many people, it is not a panacea. Donald Roberts of Bernard Haldane Associates has said that "dehired" employees must (1) be marketable, (2) have some ambition, and (3) agree to work through the company's program. Some people are convinced that they do not need these services and so choose to go it alone. Most outplacement users are in their forties or fifties and have long employment histories but are not skilled in the job-seeking process.

Those who work in outplacement are quick to correct the impression that they are high-priced employment services. Steve Merman of the Portland Management Group says, "We work on how they present themselves; we research names of contacts; we get them visible in their own profession so they come across as specialists. We get them to feel good about themselves again." They do not arrange interviews, as is typical of employment agencies; that is something the terminee does himself or herself. They also do not charge the job-seeker a fee for service.

Employers who are interested in assisting their dismissed managers and professionals have access to any number of successful otuplacement firms. To locate outplacement specialists, one need only go to the telephone directory. There are several nationwide firms with offices in the major metropolitan areas. If they are not listed under "outplacement consultants," they may be located by examining the "management consultants" heading.

Companies who choose to work with outplacement counselors do so for a number of reasons. An informal survey of typical users of these services indicated that outplacement firms are able to "take care" of people who have been valuable employees. If a company decides to change its orientation and terminates people who have been with the company twenty years, it faces a difficult dilemma. If they try to buy off the employees solely with an attractive severance package, then they abandon people whose job-seeking skills have atrophied, leaving them to flounder about on their own. When devoted employees are dumped in this way, company morale can be drastically affected.

A prominent oil-related company provides a good example of this practice. The company merged with a chemical company and needed to eliminate the duplicated management positions. When managers who had been with the company an average of twenty years were discharged and found that there would be no support past the severance package, many of those who were not fired decided to leave as well. The company, once top-heavy with experienced managers, now finds itself with a bulk of managers who have less than five years of experience. Outplacement might have averted this skill drain.

This example highlights a second reason for securing the services of an outplacement service. Maintaining employee morale is vital to the ongoing success of an organization. If those who remain are assured that the company has done all it can to assist the dismissed employee, they are more likely to hold the company in high regard. Third, while good intentions are important, companies will use outplacement when it proves financially beneficial, when it saves them money. Fourth, employees who experience the support of outplacement are less likely to sue the departed company.

While all of these goals are legitimate, it appears that outplacement is unlikely to filter down from the executive and professional ranks to non-exempt positions. Companies cannot rationalize the investment in time and money based on financial returns from the effort. Instead, the support available to dismissed employees must come from union services, local mental health professionals, ministers, family members, some government programs for retraining and employment, and other community resources.

Additionally, those employees who have been dismissed for cause, including theft and violation of rules are unlikely to receive substantial support, because of the nature of their offenses. Rehabilitation is most difficult under these circumstances. It is to the advantage of groups and organizations to which the employee belongs to develop a sensitivity to their plight and to offer assistance. Regardless, there are some who will not be helped to readjust to termination.

Federal and state employment commissions can offer some support to dismissed employees. If job hunters could receive a module or be placed in a learning center to hear tapes geared toward unemployment coping and job-seeking while they waited in line for appointments with job counselors, many who are currently alone in the process might bene-fit. Educational tools like these require substantial allocations of money and resources. Unfortunately, in difficult economic times one of the first support services usually cut is the employment commission or the human services division. A stronger commitment of local, state, and federal job agencies to adjustment could make a crucial difference to many who would not otherwise receive support.

Employers can offer a support package providing vital information to those losing jobs—referral services in the community that can direct them to additional resources, the role of employment commissions and employment agencies, ways to apply for financial support through federal programs, and tips to guide their new job search could be of some value to dismissed employees. While they may not look at the packet immediately, many might do so later on.

Economic Support

The amount of severance pay is clearly contingent on a variety of factors. The nature of the termination, the age of the employee, and the person's tenure with the company are all contributing elements to consider when determining a just severance package. In cases of rule violation, the company may feel it owes the individual nothing past the last paycheck. For employees who are near retirement the moral imperative may be enough justification for a substantial severance package. If the person has been with the company only six months, it may seem reasonable to minimize the severance, unless the person holds an expensive contract for their services.

Baytos (1972) has suggested that a percentage of annual salary, based on age, should be used for assessing the financial settlement as follows:

Age	Percentage of Annual Salary
Under 40	0
40–44	25
45–49	50
50–54	75
55–64	100

Clearly this system is weighted in favor of the long-term employee. Under Baytos's system, the executive making $70,000 at age 50 would deserve $52,000 in severance pay. Finding the person another job would more than likely be to the economic advantage of the company who has dismissed the executive. Another formula often used to determine severance pay allows a week's pay for each year served.

There are those who ask companies to consider the results of the generous severance package. Some outplacement specialists feel that large settlements serve as a disincentive rather than an incentive for reemployment. Many of those who have substantial financial support rebound more slowly from the shift than do those with smaller financial cushions.

While financial settlements may be desirable, companies may want to consider supporting the employee in ways other than direct financial remuneration. If the company can, at minimum cost, pay for health and medical insurance policies during the unemployment period, the benefits may be more important than the equivalent in dollar contributions. Each company will assess its own capacity to support terminated employees based on its own capacity to provide services.

SUMMARY

After the termination interview both managers and their former employees will experience some adjustment difficulties. Managers should take time to evaluate the interview and discover strengths and weaknesses in their approach to the dismissal. They can also direct the person to an appropriate personnel representative or counselor who can provide the assistance necessary for reentry. Companies, large and small, should consider offering support services to assist severed employees.

The employee will begin a period of reorientation in which the person's attitudes, support from family and friends, and his or her own flexibility become critical aspects of recovery. To the extent that companies can and will offer posttermination counseling, employees can explore their reactions and attempt to save face while planning a legitimate strategy for reemployment.

When the terminee is served by outplacement services, he or she can expect a positive outcome. More than 80 percent of those entering outplacement find jobs equivalent to or better than the job they left. However, it must be noted that outplacement is only available to an elite group of employees. Blue-collar or hourly workers are essentially left to their own devices. Ways to support these disenfranchised groups can be explored by local, state, and federal job agents.

Whatever else can be said, it is important to remind ourselves that dismissals do not end the moment the employee leaves the manager's office. The side effects continue for both parties for a very long time.

5

DEVELOPING STRATEGIES TO DETECT TROUBLED RELATIONSHIPS

The time-worn cliché, "An ounce of prevention is worth a pound of cure," is nowhere truer than in the termination process. We cannot calculate the numbers of dismissals which could be prevented, but it is generally accepted that the sort of relationship we develop with our subordinates affects performance. If we could reduce the number of dismissals to those that were totally unavoidable, our jobs and those of many employees would be easier in the long run. In this chapter we will identify several ways to troubleshoot problems that develop in the supervisor-subordinate relationship. If we are able to detect problem areas in these relationships early enough, then it stands to reason that we may be able to rectify situations before they become unmanageable.

To become proficient in determining whether a relationship with an employee is in jeopardy, we first must realize the significance of our informal and formal communication with the employee. A second way to place our employee relationships in perspective is by understanding how professional relationships evolve. If we can see that certain observable behaviors are present, depending on the stage of development, salvaging the relationship may be possible. Repairing difficult relationships is a challenge, but not impossible.

Informal and Formal Communication in Relationships

As we stand in the elevator or the cafeteria line, or wait by the water cooler for our turn at the fountain, surrounded by company employees, we communicate who we are in relationship to those around us. These informal exchanges contribute to the multitude of ways we are perceived. When a boss barrels into the parking lot, guns his car's motor, and slams the door, any employee who is watching will conclude that this is a day to be careful. The way we talk about our daily work, how we solve problems, how we offer advice or attempt to clarify issues demonstrate how we function in relationships. These verbal and nonverbal actions telegraph information to others.

Such informal communications, in tandem with formal employment monitoring events (the selection interview, the performance appraisal interview, and the termination interview) create environments in which human beings, be they managers or subordinates, negotiate their working relationships. Whether these formal and informal meetings yield open, productive, and honest interchanges or tight-lipped, strained, and cautious encounters depends on a multitude of factors.

Understanding How Relationships Develop

Making sense of relationships is a difficult process. We do not have a master plan to follow as we direct conversation, and a host of factors is constantly working to change the dynamics of the relationship. There are, however, certain things we have learned about relationships that can aid us in making better sense of these essential parts of our lives.

Breadth and Depth

One very telling way we can describe the supervisory relationship is to determine the extent to which we communicate with the other person. If we can talk about a variety of different topics with the subordinate, we say the communication has *breadth*. The degree to which we can discuss any single topic is considered a measure of the *depth* of communication. These terms were introduced by Altman and Taylor in their book *Social Penetration* (1973).

It is perfectly ordinary in a working environment to go to the computer trouble shooter when we need to talk about terminals that malfunction. If that is all we ever discuss with that person, then we have a relationship with a minimum of breadth but significant depth in one dimension.

Ideally, we strive for maximum comfort in our work relationships. The professional relationships we find to be the most valuable are those with seemingly limitless breadth and depth. In contrast, when our conversations with others become restricted and lack depth, we are experiencing difficulty in the relationship. It stands to reason that paying attention to the depth and breadth in our communication with others can provide us with valuable insights about the health of these important relationships.

The Stages of a Relationship

A second way of describing relationships is to understand that relationships evolve through a series of rather predictable stages. Mark Knapp (1978), an expert who studies relationships, has developed a model to explain how relationships grow and deteriorate. The model identifies ten different stages in human relationships, taking us from initiation to termination.

For our purposes, his system of relational stages has been adapted for the business and professional environment in Figure 5-1. Recognizing these stages in our relationships with subordinates can help us to determine how to improve the situation. There is no predetermined time frame for each stage, and many relationships do not progress through all ten stages. Most seesaw back and forth, attempting to maintain a semblance of stability.

It is possible to interpret these stages as inevitable, one leading always to another. In our own experiences we know this is simply not true. Stage 6, differentiating, for example, is a common stage representing disagreement. We frequently move from bonding to differentiating and back to bonding. This is a healthy function of growing relationships. In the difficult relationship individuals may view the conflict and recognition

Figure 5-1

Supervisor-Subordinate Relationship Stages

STAGE	JOB-RELATED BEHAVIOR
1. Initiating	Recruitment of employee; initial contact through the application process.
2. Experimenting	Interviewing and hiring or dismissing the individual. Probationary period allows the manager and the employee to determine if the job fit is a good one. Employee knows the temporary contractual nature of the employment.
3. Intensifying	The probationary period ends. The employee has the sense that the organization has sanctioned the employment.
4. Integrating	The employee becomes a functioning part of the organization. He or she picks up company jargon, becomes a member of company cliques, and is a walking ambassador for the company. The employee identifies with the company.
5. Bonding	The employer acknowledges the worth of the employee, providing additional incentives to continue the relationship. The employee feels secure in the stability of the work relationship and invests unsolicited energy into the organization.

(left margin label: GROWTH STAGES)

Adapted from models developed by Mark Knapp, *Social Intercourse: From Greeting to Goodbye* and Irving Altman and Taylor, *Social Penetration.*

CHARACTERISTICS OF THE STAGE

We scan the other person, considering our own stereotypes and prior knowledge of the person's reputation as well as our expectations for the situation. This stage is affected by the time available, where you are meeting, and the special rituals appropriate to the occasion.

We attempt to discover the unknown, seeking common ground and exchanging basic information. This stage is affected by the degree of interest both parties show, the capacity of both to engage in small talk, and the extent of mutual satisfaction with the exchange. In many instances termination occurs in this stage.

The relationship builds. One or both parties will ask favors of the other; forms of address may become more informal; "we" becomes more frequent than "I"; both parties know each other well enough that they no longer need to complete all of their statements. They begin to make statements of commitment: "We have a dynamite team here." They are willing to help the other be understood by saying, "In other words, you mean . . ."

A true partnership develops around the uniqueness of the duo. They engage in more joint projects and share possessions. Work attitudes are similar.

Formal contractual commitments are publicly announced. Becoming a partner or a valued member of the staff is taken for granted.

Figure 5-1 *(continued)*

STAGE	JOB-RELATED BEHAVIOR
6. Differentiating	The employer and employee may begin to separate belongings and time ("My time" versus "company time"). The individual's perception of his or her place in the hierarchy may change. Job dissatisfaction creeps into the working relationship. Fault-finding in job performances may occur. There is a slight sense of inequity.
7. Circumscribing	The information exchanged between employer and employee is reduced significantly. The employee may notice that information routinely channeled to him or her is not available. Both reduce the amount of time spent on casual conversation. The employee may begin to feel the organization does not deserve his or her investment.
8. Stagnating	The employer/employee begin to mark time. Either or both parties engage in behavior barely sufficient to maintain a communication linkage. Speaking occurs in obligatory situations.
9. Avoiding	Employer/employee interactions are brief and reflect the desire of at least one party to diminish the time and energy spent in the relationship. Long lunches, long absences, preferences for jobs sanctioned outside of the normal workplace, failure to respond to memos, or delaying work are all part of this stage. This condition can linger if action to redirect the person is not taken.
10. Terminating	One party takes the initiative to end the relationship. (In the firing process it is the manager; in resignations, action is taken by the employee.)

DECAY STAGES (bracketing stages 6–10)

CHARACTERISTICS OF THE STAGE

In this first stage of disengagement there is a focus on individual differences. Conflict becomes apparent and each party recognizes that the other is imperfect.

Messages sent are very controlled, regulating the topics of communication. Both breadth and depth are diminished. Superficiality is present; self-disclosure has severely diminished. "Nothing" and "None of your business" may become common replies.

There is nothing new in the relationship. It seems frozen. The unknown is fallaciously considered known. Each may feel, "There is no sense in bringing this up because I know what you'll say."

Reduction of face-to-face or telephone contact accelerates. The parties make excuses for not seeing each other.

Both parties are preparing to function without the other. Termination dialog will be affected by the type of relationship they have had, the status differences, the amount of time allowed, and the type of relationship desired in the future.

of self versus the other as a reason to progress toward disintegration. In healthy relationships both parties perceive the bond between the two as strong enough to weather the temporary turbulence. In the decaying relationship the frustration is viewed as proof of the incompatibility of the two parties. There is a growing sense that "we simply cannot work together." This could be translated into, "I no longer think the rewards I am getting from this situation are adequate" or "I am unwilling to work to rebuild this relationship."

Using the model   In using the model of supervisory-subordinate relationships in Figure 5-1, it is important to think about our own relationships with employees. For a moment, mentally identify the people who work for and with you. How many of these relationships are satisfying working partnerships? Ask yourself how each relationship fits into the model. It may be helpful to draw a continuum line for ourselves and another parallel to it for each employee, as in Figure 5-2.

This process lets us visually picture our perceptions of the linkage between ourselves and our employees. It assists us in understanding that some employees will remain in the bonding stage until they receive gold watches; others will see better opportunities for themselves in other organizations or other careers; and others will be dismissed for a host of reasons. The model will allow some of us to identify trouble spots in our relationships with employees so that remedial action can be taken. It can also be used to explain why some terminations are more awkward and painful than others.

Stage incompatibility   One of the interesting possibilities that complicates the supervisory-subordinate relationship is the chance that each person may be in a different stage of growth or decay. For instance, the employee who perceives herself in the bonding stage and is pleased with her performance, having received little criticism of her abilities, will be overwhelmed by the news that her manager is considering termination of her services. If the employee's level of dissatisfaction moves toward termination at the same time as the employer's, then chances are a resignation will result, not a firing. Still other conditions are possible. Managers sometimes find themselves startled to discover that an employee is looking for another job, because they were pleased and optimistic about the person's place in the organization.

Paying attention to these stages can help to explain, for instance, why the layoff is such a painful type of termination. First, the employee and the employer may be in the intensifying and bonding stages. Second, there may not be a natural flow of disenchantment. Third, there seems to be no real tangible enemy. The sudden death of the relationship may catapult the manager and the subordinate into a state of disorientation. There is a sense that the rug has been pulled out from under them.

As you identify the relative positions of your subordinates in the ten evolutionary stages shown in Figure 5-2, take into account the evidence you have that would verify your approximation. Also note the variance between all the employee stages you have estimated. Is there a wide range or a narrow range?

Figure 5-2
Supervisory-Subordinate Relationship Worksheet

	Initiating Stage	Experimenting Stage	Intensifying Stage	Integrating Stage	Bonding Stage	Differentiating Stage	Circumscribing Stage	Stagnating Stage	Avoiding Stage	Terminating Stage
My View	1	2	3	4	5	6	7	8	9	10
Employee 1	1	2	3	4	5	6	7	8	9	10
My View	1	2	3	4	5	6	7	8	9	10
Employee 2	1	2	3	4	5	6	7	8	9	10
My View	1	2	3	4	5	6	7	8	9	10
Employee 3	1	2	3	4	5	6	7	8	9	10
My View	1	2	3	4	5	6	7	8	9	10
Employee 4	1	2	3	4	5	6	7	8	9	10
My View	1	2	3	4	5	6	7	8	9	10
Employee 5	1	2	3	4	5	6	7	8	9	10

Because the natural cycle is violated in a layoff, the employer cannot be easily blamed for the decision, but he or she can certainly be vulnerable regarding how the termination was handled. Layoffs tend to reinforce the sense of the manager as a "gutless wonder" who sends the message in the pay envelope or calls a meeting at 4:30 p.m. on a Friday afternoon to tell everyone about the plant shutdown.

Another awkward situation develops when the person who is dismissed has developed a loyal following. In one academic dismissal, the assistant director of an educational literacy project was fired by her boss. The assistant director had reported evidence of graft and abuse of government funds to her boss's superiors and had been assured that her whistle-blowing was an important action that would not affect her standing with the university. Her staff supported her actions and resented the project director. Within six months of the firing, 83% of the staff for the project voluntarily resigned, leaving the project in jeopardy. After six months of legal negotiations, the assistant project director was reinstated with back pay on the condition that she resign. The strength of the relational bonds between the assistant director and her workforce demonstrate the power of human interactions to affect the destiny of work projects.

Without getting involved in the ethical questions that cases like the whistle-blowing situation raise, some general conclusions about the relationships involved can be reached by using the model of relationship stages. When the assistant director found troublesome records that could not be justified and expenses that were claimed under several different accounts, she moved from bonding to differentiating. The more evidence she found, the further away from bonding and the closer to termination she pushed.

The project director's reaction can also be explained in the same manner. His satisfaction with the assistant director's performance moved from bonding almost immediately to termination when he discovered she had talked with his superiors about her findings. His defensive reaction was to eliminate the source of discomfort and threat. His position was in jeopardy. Breaches like this make it almost impossible for amicable reconciliations to occur—although miracles have been known to happen.

The Quality of Communication

A third way to describe how we function with our employees requires us to watch how we talk to them. The words and gestures we use in this process are telling. They characterize the quality of the business relationship. Typically, we can tell the difference between a warm greeting and a cool reception, but we do not know what we should attribute it to. Let us examine seven different ways to test the quality of the working relationship by asking simple questions.

1. Are you feeling that the range of safe topics keeps narrowing? Participants in growing, effective relationships can discuss a variety of topics. Whether praise or criticism is involved, there is a sense that every idea will receive a fair hearing. In the narrow case, there is a feeling of tension related to many topics. It may feel like walking through a mine field, looking for safe spots that are not booby-trapped. Either or both parties may refuse to talk to each other. Communication is described as closed. When the communication between two people narrows, we can look for ways to broaden it.

2. Do you talk to others in a way that lets them know you value them as individuals? When relationships begin to deteriorate we communicate in a less personal way, using a stylized approach. The communication is rife with clichés. The other party begins to feel more like a piece of furniture and less like a human being. We rely on patterns rather than making specific references about shared experiences. "This is company policy. It has always been this way. There is no reason to change now," instead of, "I know some policies don't always seem to make sense, but there are some reasons why we have chosen to do it this way. Let me explain them to you."

3. Does it take a lot of energy to get your messages across? Is it hard to know what to say? When we cannot predict the likely reactions of others because we are communicating less openly, interactions are more difficult and less efficient. This degree of difficulty creates discomfort and shuts down the desire to communicate.

4. Are you free to communicate with the other person through all available channels? When we relate flexibly with others we are free to use all possible channels at our disposal. We do not hesitate to chat face-to-face or over the telephone, using our most versatile repertoire of words and body gestures. If we find we prefer to communicate in remote ways—through memos or other people—the relationship is taking on a more rigid tone. Rigidity also implies that we may easily lose the ability to sense the subtle shades of meaning in messages the other sends.

5. Do you notice awkward silences and false starts and stops in your communication? When people are relating well to each other, they function like dancing partners who easily and smoothly follow one another. Power struggles do not exist. The relationship in trouble is punctuated by awkward silences and false starts and stops, almost as though you have never met the person before. It might be called "becoming strangers again".

6. Do you find that you no longer share the reporting of your daily concerns with the other and vice versa? When we enjoy the benefits of a growing relationship, there is typically a willingness to reveal our likes and dislikes. If, however, we are becoming more wary of the other person,

it is natural to limit the disclosures we make to the other to information that is public instead of private.

7. Is there a hesitancy in the relationship? Relationships that are spontaneous, where appointments need not be made, where there is an easy give and take, tend to satisfy both parties. In contrast, when every move feels guarded and paranoia edges into the perception of the relationship, the relationship is on a downturn.

The chart in Figure 5-3 provides an easy reference for these characteristics of growing and decaying relationships. As in the Knapp (1978) model of relationship stages, each description is not complete in and of itself. These qualities in the communication are symptomatic of healthy, effective working relationships or of relationships in need of help. They are used to verify our perceptions of our business communication with our subordinates.

Our communication with employees can serve as a safety valve to prevent some possible terminations and encourage others that are necessary. When we communicate to reinforce the positive aspects of these relationships we are confirming the other person. Confirmation may take the form of listening attentively, questioning, clarifying, agreeing, and recognizing the uniqueness of each employee. These skills reflect a desire to communicate with the other and attach a certain importance to the relationship.

On the other hand, if we find ourselves ignoring the subordinate, making disparaging comments about him or her, responding to the person in conflicting ways, treating him or her as an inanimate object, this disconfirming method of relating is heading us for trouble. In general

Figure 5-3
Moving Toward Growth or Decay

TOWARD GROWTH	TOWARD DECAY
Breadth	Narrowness
Uniqueness	Stylized
Efficiency	Difficulty
Flexibility	Rigidity
Smoothness	Awkwardness
Personal	Public
Spontaneity	Hesitancy

we all like to be recognized rather than ignored, to be treated personally rather than impersonally, to be taken seriously rather than discounted as tangential.

SUMMARY

As we think about our own communication abilities, it is unrealistic to assume that these skills can or will make terminations easy. Learning to describe how we relate to our subordinates by examining the breadth and depth in our communication, noticing which stage we find ourselves in the relationship, and clarifying the quality of our communication with our subordinate offer us criteria for assessing whether a relationship can be rehabilitated or must end.

The importance of preventive maintenance cannot be discounted. When relationships are in trouble in the office, there are clear signals of trouble in the communication between managers and their subordinates. Simply cultivating an awareness of these danger signals can alert managers to troubled relationships, giving them time to initiate remedial actions.

6

WHAT MAKES IT SO HARD?

> The thought of change is a *dream.*
> The *fear* of change is unhealthy.
> The need of change is *mandatory.*
> The result of change is *acceptance.*
> —Anonymous (1976)

This short epithet takes us through the essence of the termination process. Before terminations occur there are a variety of different dreams, some good, some bad. The next ingredient, fear, promises to negatively affect the dismissal, stimulating guilt and anger about the unknown future. Action then follows, bringing about the essential change in the relationship between manager and subordinate. Eventually, the action is accepted by all parties, although not necessarily at the same time.

In a candid moment, Chris, a nursing supervisor, admitted that she spent more time fearing her first termination interview than she did her first budget review or any other personnel action she had taken. In asking what makes termination interviewing so hard, we have to examine the human factors involved.

Fear and Forgiveness

In this chapter, our human responses to conflict, defensiveness, and change will be explored as they interact with the termination event. One of these very human responses which can help us understand the way we relate to dismissal is fear. Fear heightens our defensive reactions to the delicate developments in the interview of dismissal, and distorts our understanding of the change process.

In his best-selling book, *Love Is Letting Go of Fear,* Dr. Gerald Jampolsky (1981) examines the results we reap when we function out of fear. Jampolsky, founder of a counseling center for terminally ill children and their parents, has taught hundreds of people to approach loss events without fear. Dismissals surely count as loss events in both human and financial terms. Understanding the Jampolsky vision of fear enables us to view the termination event in a more productive way.

An important question we can ask ourselves is, how does fear become a primary motivator for managers in dismissals? We may function out of fear if:

- We are worried about what the employee will say to us, so we postpone the action.
- Our foremost concern is whether or not the individual will sue us or the company.

- We have a need to attack the record and behavior of the employee to justify the termination.

- We become defensive or feel threatened by questions raised by the terminee or other managers.

- We feel that the employee has made a fool of us or has taken advantage of our generosity; we see ourselves as victims.

- Our thoughts are riveted on guilt that we feel, either for failure to act soon enough or for failure to clarify problems.

- Anger surfaces and we begin to feel that the person has dis- appointed us personally.

- We hired the person and blame ourselves for a poor decision.

It is the rare manager who has not felt at least one of these feelings. Many of them seem conflicting; others may seem completely legitimate. If we are plagued by our own fear of failure or fear of the other's actions, or if we see the dismissal as the ruination of a career, the termination process promises to be more difficult. If many of us associate the termination process with some degree of fear, what must we do in order to perceive the dismissal from a more productive vantage point?

To begin with, we have to accept that the action *must* occur, under- standing that at the present moment dismissal is the only legitimate course of action. With this acceptance in mind, Jampolsky suggests that fear can be combatted through acts of forgiveness. When we are fear- ful we hold onto grievances, dissatisfaction, and frustration. It is only through a process of letting go of these injustices that we are able to free ourselves of the fear that underlies many of the feelings mentioned on the previous page.

To achieve this degree of detachment from the dismissal, Jampolsky recommends absolute clemency. We forgive ourselves for any mistakes we have made with the employee, we forgive the employee for his or her failures, and we forgive the situation for all its inequities. Forgiveness is a necessary condition of acceptance. Forgiveness is also a precursor to effective rational decision making. When we as managers function out of fear, our thinking processes may become cloudy and actions may evolve for all the wrong reasons. Ridding ourselves of fear, then, is necessary for handling the termination process wisely.

How can we put forgiveness into practice? Looking at a real case may help us clarify its importance and illustrate the challenge involved in arriving at a state of emotional and rational balance.

A large hotel chain's manager in the Midwest, John, reported that he was caught in a classic bind between a newly promoted female employee and his upper-echelon male managers. John had promoted Mrs. King to assistant manager because he knew that with the right training and some patience, she would become a first-rate manager. She was a loyal and trustworthy person who had always managed to come through for him in a pinch.

John's attempt to support the promotion of women into management in his chain backfired. His promotion of Mrs. King was greeted in the higher echelons with cold acknowledgment. At every point the managers made their displeasure with John's decision known. Mrs. King made what John considered, understandable mistakes—mistakes that any novice manager could have made. The higher-ups saw these blunders and leapt on them as proof of incompetence. While John was away on vacation, the front-office managers descended upon Mrs. King, declaring that she was not long for the job because of her poor record.

When John returned he was faced with an ultimatum to fire her. He was furious. They had not given her a chance, had not allowed him to follow through as he had wanted. He suspected that the real reason he was pressured to dismiss Mrs. King was grounded in his boss' preference for male managers. He postponed the termination until he could wait no longer. In truth there would be nothing but trouble ahead for Mrs. King if she remained in the position. Clearly the attitudes at headquarters were not going to change. Only in acting could he hope that Mrs. King would take some legal action challenging the unbending attitudes toward women managers. In order to work with his superiors he had to forgive them of their blindness, he had to forgive himself for having promoted Mrs. King into the furor, and had to forgive her for making the predictable mistakes that allowed the managers to nail her. Once he had realized that Mrs. King would function much better in an environment that could support her as a woman manager, the termination interview took on a different tone.

To even the casual observer the facts in this case point to at least a potential violation of sex discrimination legislation. The dilemma for the manager arises out of the conflict between his feelings of injustice, his own job security, and his concern for the future of Mrs. King's career. He felt angry with his superiors, afraid for his own job stability, and guilty about how the entire event had been handled. While he was caught up in this emotional upheaval, he could not handle the procedures leading to termination. Only when he recognized that the situation had deteriorated to such a point that Mrs. King could never function in a way that would please the superiors, that she could never trust them to treat her fairly, and that the action was essential, could he act in good conscience.

Most of us would experience the same feelings as John. It is actually arriving at the point of acceptance of the dismissal that presents so many problems for us. One explanation for our difficulties in arriving at the termination action has to do with the ways in which we view conflict.

Conflict

Practically from birth, we have witnessed a variety of attitudes toward human conflict. We have seen people operate from a variety of different vantage points: successful and unsuccessful, honest and dishonest, healthy and unhealthy. Just as the way we cope with fear in our lives affects the way we approach terminations, so does the way we react to conflict.

Arguments, fights, disagreements, differences of opinion—even free-for-all—are all terms that indicate conflict between people. In terminations most of us expect that there will be a difference of opinion regarding the decision to terminate, creating a me-versus-you attitude. While this adversarial viewpoint may materialize, it is by no means certain. Conflict can be defined as a condition existing between two people when each views the other's ideas or attitudes as barriers to obtaining what he or she wants. When a struggle exists, it usually develops because one party has something that the other wants.

When we view our goals as incompatible and engage in conflict with others, we are competing in some way for scarce rewards; it becomes possible to see the other person as interfering with our achievement of a goal. From the manager's standpoint, an employee who is not producing quality work can be evaluated as uninterested in the goal of quality production, interfering with the accomplishment of higher productivity levels, and reducing the chance to generate more scarce rewards (profits). The worker can view the same situation in different terms. She or he may feel that the manager only cares about numbers and production quotas and doesn't care about the worker. She or he can only work productively in a supportive environment, so the manager is blamed for the reduction in productivity. Scarce resources for the employee may take on the meaning of positive comments to the worker from the manager. In a standard conflict both parties are likely to see the other as wrong or at fault. It is because each has difficulty understanding the other's position that negotiation can be stymied.

Why does conflict present such an obstacle to managers? It may not, in fact, be the conflict itself but rather the fear of it that actually creates the difficulty. If we believe any number of myths about conflict being abnormal, evil, pathological, or inevitably hostile then it is no wonder we shy away from it. Typically, it is the way we behave when conflict emerges that defines our attitude toward it. Books abound that describe conflict management. Authors Filley (1975) and Frost and Wilmot (1978) have studied the phenomenon of conflict and suggest that there are some standard strategies that we choose when confronted with such a struggle.

Avoiding Conflict

Perhaps one of the most familiar methods of dealing with conflict is to attempt to avoid it. You may have heard the story of the man who patiently, for twenty years, ate toast and jelly for breakfast every morning because his wife fixed it. He did not like it, but did not want to cause any trouble. Some of us will go to great lengths to avoid even the faintest possibility of conflict. Avoidance can be viewed negatively or positively. If we are refusing to deal with the issues, then we are relating negatively to conflict. If, on the other hand, we have chosen to refrain from confronting the issue because we cannot win, then we may be realistically assessing the situation and responding positively. When the other person is in a state of confusion induced by a sudden barrage of unpredicted events, for instance, he or she is not in a frame of mind in which problem solving and confronting issues can be productive. Of course, the validity of this analysis depends on our own capacity to rationalize our behavior. We may feel that we are functioning positively when in fact we are simply shying away from conflict.

It is not just individuals who avoid conflict. Chester Burger (1972), a management consultant and author of *Creative Firing,* tells of a large company planning a move to the Sun Belt that notified its employees on a Friday afternoon that the move would occur beginning the following week. To find out whether they would be moved or fired, employees were to call the switchboard and ask the operator to locate their names on one of two lists. In this way the managers felt they would sneak out of town by using "go" and "stay" lists. Such avoidance of problem-solving discussions can generate a lot of hostility. Such a move sets a precedent for underhanded action that may backfire, even to those selected to make the move. Avoidance speaks volumes to those affected.

Dismissals also invite cowardice and avoidance of conflict. When we enclose a slip of paper in someone's paycheck notifying him or her that the job has been eliminated, we practice avoidance. In the extreme case, managers have been known to avoid terminating someone because the possibility of unpleasantness was so abhorrent. Just as managers have a preferred conflict management strategy, so do their employees. When both parties are most comfortable avoiding conflict, decision making necessarily suffers. It should be noted that our particular conflict style is situational and varies based on the nature of the relationship we have with the other person.

With a very quiet, well-meaning employee we may be able to calmly address the issues in the termination and respond clearly to the person's reaction. However, belligerent employee behavior may intimidate us so that we avoid the issue by soft-peddling it. Or we may overreact, using inflammatory language that fuels additional anger. The avoidance of conflict may take many forms. In Figure 6-1 you will find some of the typical ways people avoid conflict.

There are times when we avoid conflict because we are afraid of losing. Such an attitude, if it is the dominant mode of responding to conflict, becomes a self-fulfilling prophecy. We may say to ourselves, "I never win arguments, so I should not bring it up." It is possible that we never win because we never really deal with the issues openly and honestly.

Figure 6-1
Roles for Avoiding Conflict

The following roles are designed to avoid creating an open, supportive climate, making legitimate problem-solving impossible. These methods annoy others and might be called "crazy makers."

Avoider: Refuses to fight. A conflict is the signal for this individual to leave, physically if not in spirit.

Pseudoaccommodator: Refuses to fight and pretends nothing is wrong. This role usually increases hostility, aggression, and conflict.

Subject changer: Escapes conflict by changing the topic to a more neutral one. This keeps the other from interacting in the problem area, generating solutions, and possibly resolving the problem.

Criticizer: Attacks the other on a personal level to avoid expressing his or her own feelings.

Gunnysacker: Avoids dealing with a problem at the time it arises by putting the hostility and resentment generated in a "gunny sack," allowing them to accumulate.

Joker: Refuses to take any problem seriously. This keeps the other person from exploring the sources of the conflict, and also increases hostility toward the person enacting this role.

Blamer: Refuses to work on solving the conflict, preferring to assign blame to someone else. This role causes the other person to become extremely defensive.

Withholder: Refuses to deal with the conflict, but instead punishes the other by withholding something of value.

Benedict Arnold: Refuses to deal with the conflict and punishes the other by sabotage, selling out, or giving away secrets.

From Rosenfeld (1976)

Forcing

Many of us grew up with the overriding sense that bosses have to be strong. Being strong, of course, has a close companion, being right. The drive to be strong and right in a termination interview suggests a "forcing" view of conflict. We may say to ourselves, "At all costs, I will win and you will lose." The termination becomes a game of skill and dexterity. There are indeed a variety of underhanded ways to ensure that we will win and the other person lose. We might develop a strategy that encourages a shouting match or use tactics guaranteed to intimidate the other, either by inundating the other person with facts or by making unfair observations about the person's character or upbringing. We might present information at an awkward time for the subordinate or in an awkward place, not giving time to think about it. Finally, we might spring the message on the person with no warning.

The "I win–you lose" attitude that underlies this method is often triggered in many of us when we feel our egos have been threatened. For others, it is a standard part of our personality. The authoritarian nature of the forcing approach to conflict may elicit a variety of employee reactions in the termination interview. The employee may respond more violently than normal because of the perceived "unfairness" of the style. Also common is a passive-aggressive reaction in which the employee seems to cower under the power of the manager, but is seething with vengefulness on the inside. Many employees will attempt to steal company possessions more readily when they feel they have not been treated properly. Such gestures may be more symbolic than expensive. Stealing all of the yogurt out of the company refrigerator or taking staplers and tape dispensers may be viewed as "just what I am owed." Companies that proudly say, "we never have to fire anyone; we make life so uncomfortable for them that they leave," are functioning from a position of ruthlessness and forcing.

A leasing company, trying to get rid of a middle-aged sales manager, exemplifies this attitude. Bill, a very successful salesman, had recently joined the staff of a rapidly expanding leasing firm in the western states. The company, while it realized that the man's contacts in leasing could be valuable to them, began to hint that they wanted younger men in the sales force. Bill's sales figures were exactly what he had promised, sometimes higher, but the company was mobilizing to force him to resign. The president of the company flew to the western headquarters and "chewed Bill out for six hours." Witnesses were appalled at the executive temper tantrum. When Bill joined the company he had asked for policy and procedures manuals; the guides were not forthcoming. When the main office sent letter after letter saying procedures used in the western office were all wrong, Bill asked for models that would allow his office to conform to other regions. He never received further instruction.

Bill filed an age discrimination suit against the company; not long after the suit was filed the company president notified Bill of his immediate termination. The attitudes toward conflict exemplified in this case support the "might is right" mentality. Forcing is akin to that time-honored behavior—bullying. As in the previous example, the forcing style rarely identifies the true issues of the termination. The company tried to condemn Bill for not following procedures, yet would not provide them. When a business functions from such a tenuous ethical basis, clarifying the honest reasons for termination would drag it into an expensive legal battle. Instead, the firm chose to take the risk of manipulating the issues, hoping that nothing would come of its actions.

Compromising

Some of us have been taught that we must give in enough to settle an issue. Compromising can mean that we meet the other person half-way. In termination interviewing, this is a difficult position to negotiate from. The manager who untiringly compromises may wind up giving the subordinate his or her job back. The overriding view of conflict is that "I will win some and you will lose some, while I will lose some and you will win some." While this sense of reciprocity is admirable, it can also be troublesome in the interview itself. It is based on the premise of fairness. At times we assume that since we cannot get what we want, half a loaf is better than none. It is from this modified defeatist position that compromise can arise. Many times, the assumption is false—often we could get what we want.

As evidenced by the sincere difficulties encountered by labor and management negotiators who seek to compromise, negotiation in this mode is delicate and time-consuming.

Smoothing

The image that comes to mind with the smoothing style is one of smoothing ruffled feathers. There is a slight suggestion that a kindly grandparent might be calming our anger by gently patting us on the back and saying, "There, there. It isn't as bad as all that." The smoothing style can be a valuable enabling style to use in conjunction with problem solving. If the goal of the smoother is to reduce the emotional turmoil prior to legitimate negotiation, then it may serve an extremely useful function. However, it is possible for the smoothing style to foster avoidance and withdrawal as easily as it prepares us for confronting the true issues in a conflict.

Whether smoothing serves to promote avoidance or confrontation depends on the motivation of the individual using the style. Just as a knife in the hands of a skilled surgeon can save lives, that same knife in the hands of a vicious criminal can end lives. The style, like the knife, depends on the user for its eventual effect. Smoothing can mean the individual has adopted a tolerant attitude toward the other party to the conflict, believing that "kind words are worth much and cost little." If the person has learned that calming people down and diverting their attention from the issue sometimes allows the conflict to die down momentarily, the smoothing strategy can be used to help others forget the real issues at hand.

Confronting

The connotations the word "confronting" holds in our minds are often colored by thoughts of aggression. In this context, however, confronting should be viewed as a problem-solving and issue-oriented approach. As conflict strategies, both avoiding and forcing often disregard the issues themselves. By confronting the issues, we remove from the process the need to protect our egos and our own fear of loss. While all issues cannot be solved or changed through problem-solving efforts, they can at least be better understood. A primary goal of confronting is the development of a mutual understanding of the conflict and the choices that are available to the parties involved.

We are more likely to function from a confrontational style when we understand that each person has legitimate reasons for feeling and thinking as he or she does. While we may not agree, we at least accept that the other's position is legitimate; the issue of who is right need never enter into the dialogue. Instead, we focus on arriving at the most effective and satisfying solution to the difficulty.

In the termination interview, something that cannot be negotiated is the finality of the termination decision. What can be confronted is the rationale for the decision, the legitimacy of the employee's human reaction to the message, and the question of what support the employee can expect from the manager and the company.

More than anything else, the confronting style is an outward and visible sign of an inner condition of stability. The style suggests that the person is capable of coping with and benefitting from the truth. In its purest form, confronting reveals the maturity of the individual.

Observations About Conflict

The confronting style may be one we would aspire toward as an ideal. One constraint that often makes confronting difficult is the style employed by the other party or parties. It is relatively easy to discuss an issue with another who is of the same mind. On the contrary, when the other party insists "there is nothing wrong," or that "you're all wet!," bringing the talk back to a problem-solving mode may not be a possibility. Under circumstances where the other party refuses to engage in constructive problem-solving, it is important to assess what can be done to salvage the situation.

It can be important to listen to the other person's reaction and analysis, serving as a fact-finder. Clarifying confusing procedures and practices may be valuable. We must accept that the other person in a termination interview may not be psychologically capable of engaging in problem solving at the time of the interview. Emotional reactions may impair the process significantly.

Another observation we may need to be reminded of is the ongoing nature of our attitudes toward conflict. Our attitudes toward conflict influence our relationship with the other person from the moment he or she is hired to the moment of dismissal. The termination interview is merely the culmination of the dynamic that has developed throughout our time with the employee.

While few of us want to be viewed by our subordinates as the company ogre, many of us are attached to the desire that our employees like us. It is difficult for someone we terminate to like us. The rejection implicit in a termination makes friendly exchanges less likely. It is important for managers to recognize that employees may or may not like us when we initiate an action as painful as dismissal. Often the manager serves as the whipping boy for the departed employee. On some occasions, the employee may recognize that the manager was doing his or her job and still respect the manager. The desire to be liked becomes an important issue, especially if it immobilizes the manager in the decision-making process. If he or she makes a decision for the sole purpose of maintaining popularity, without consideration for organizational goals and effectiveness, that decision is going to cause trouble.

It is important to notice that the conflict styles described in this chapter are not mutually exclusive. While I may prefer to confront with one person, another may bring out the forcing style in me. Still others may prompt me to compromise or avoid the issue entirely.

Select the statements below that you feel most often represent your attitudes toward conflict. This will give you an idea of your preferred conflict style.

1. It is easier to refrain than to retreat from a quarrel.
2. If you cannot make a person think as you do, make him or her do as you think.
3. Soft words win warm hearts.

4. You scratch my back, I'll scratch yours.

5. Come now and let us reason together.

Each of the conflict styles discussed refers to general patterns of behavior.* Understanding the dynamics of a manager-subordinate interaction requires paying attention to the specific messages that each party sends to the other. These messages originate from the attitudes we hold toward conflict (see Figure 6-2).

The figure also suggests that the specific messages we send to others may fall into one of two categories, defensive or supportive messages. Clarifying how our attitudes and the messages we send interact is valuable, in that we recognize they are not independent of one another. The message is an outward and vocal sign of our inner state of mind. In the next section of this chapter we are asked to consider the nature of the messages we send in the termination interview. Are we sending messages that promote defensiveness in others or messages that produce supportive responses in others?

Figure 6-2
Attitudes Toward Conflict

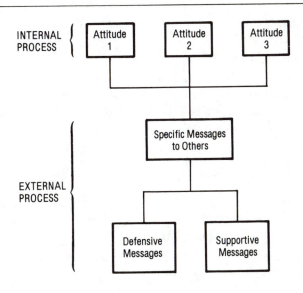

---

* 1–Avoiding 2–Forcing 3–Smoothing 4–Compromising 5–Confronting

Defensive and Supportive Messages

The interview of dismissal is a natural holding tank for ego-protecting communication. Each party wants to save face, but the way our conflict attitudes manifest themselves in our communication can intensify the natural defensiveness that is built into the dismissal situation. Common sense tells us that we are more likely to become defensive when we feel rejected or fear the outcome of any predicament. Terminations satisfy both conditions: they involve rejection and they are unpredictable. To develop a better sense of what messages make others defensive, examine the list of comments below and determine for yourself which you feel would make you react more negatively or defensively.

1. "Everything you touch gets screwed up!"

   <or>

   "I'm concerned that the deadlines we set for the turn-around in your performance have not been met."

2. "I've told you and told you and told you not to do it this way."

   <or>

   "There are some important reasons why I think mistakes continue to be made in your job."

3. "I think we can both see you would be happier somewhere else, wouldn't you?"

   <or>

   "I think, under the circumstances, you have done the best that you can do. Unfortunately, our needs have changed as a company and we are moving in a different direction. That direction, unfortunately does not demand your skills."

4. "When a person can't cut the mustard he usually knows it, doesn't he?"

   <or>

   "I understand this must come as a shock to you; in the past you have given us good work. The last eight months there's been a falling off in your performance."

5. "I've been supervising line operators for fifteen years, son. Nobody talks to me like that."

   <or>

   "Everyone makes mistakes. This one cost us a lot of money. We have to take action, because we cannot afford mistakes like this. I hope you can understand our predicament."

6. "I don't want to hear your excuses. I have made this decision and I'm sticking to it."

   <or>

   "I'm sure you feel that we've made a bad decision. Given the circumstances we have done the best we knew how to do. We simply cannot give you another chance."

7. "Look, it's not my fault we have to let you go. We were all told to reduce force and you just happen to be the one with the least seniority. It's a tough break."

   <or>

   "I want you to understand how this decision was made. The company is experiencing a financial loss and we have to reduce the size of our payroll. In cases like this, each of us had to identify two people in our group with the least seniority. It just happens, John, that you were hired three months after Cynthia and Bill."

If you recognized the defensive elements in these seven examples, you selected the first statement in each category as an example of negative or defensive communication. As early as 1961, Jack Gibb, a research psychologist, developed a system to help us identify those elements of messages that encourage us to perceive them as defensive or antagonistic. Gibb was also able to describe the supportive elements of messages that tend to reinforce and balance the listener. In Figure 6-3 you will find each of the six defensive communication characteristics and their supportive counterparts.

Examining the Gibb system can provoke us to evaluate our own messages. But how do we determine whether our messages to others meet his criteria for defensive behavior? We can start by asking ourselves whether our attitudes toward the person to be dismissed, the situation creating the dismissal, and the workplace in general reflect the need to evaluate others, control their behavior, manipulate the situation to our advantage, treat others as objects, feel that we are in some way better than others, or be in a position that is always right. On the other hand, we may ask ourselves if in approaching the dismissal we have made every effort to focus on factual and nonjudgmental descriptions of events, our desire to solve the problem with the other person, natural expression of our concerns, respect for the other person as a human being, acceptance of the other person or the situation regardless of differences in position, personality, or ability, or willingness to negotiate with the other person from a flexible frame of reference.

To test these attitudes that serve as the basis for the messages we send, answer the questions regarding the last termination interview you conducted.

Figure 6-3

Defensive and Supportive Communication

Defensive	Supportive
1. Evaluation: To pass moral judgment on another; to blame or praise; make moral assessments of another or question his/her motives; to question the other's standards.	1. Description: Nonjudgmental; to ask questions which are perceived as requests for information; to present feelings, emotions, events which do not ask the other to change behavior.
2. Control: To try to do something to another; to attempt to change behavior or attitudes of others; implicit in attempts to change others is the assumption that they are inadequate.	2. Problem orientation: To convey a desire to collaborate in solving a mutual problem or defining it; to allow the other to set his/her goals and solve his/her own problem; to imply that you do not desire to impose your solution.
3. Strategy: To manipulate another into thinking he/she was making his/her own decisions; to engage in multiple and/or ambiguous motivations; to treat the other as a guinea pig.	3. Spontaneity: To express naturalness; free of deception; a "clean id"; straightforwardness; uncomplicated motives.
4. Neutrality: To express a lack of concern for the other; the clinical, person-as-object-of-study attitude.	4. Empathy: To respect the other person and show it; to take his/her role; to identify with his/her problems; to share his/her feelings.
5. Superiority: To communicate that you are superior in position, wealth, intelligence, etc.; to arouse feelings of inadequacy in others; to express that you are unwilling to enter into joint problem solving.	5. Equality: To be willing to enter into participative planning with mutual trust and respect; to attach little importance to differences in ability, worth, status, etc.
6. Certainty: To be dogmatic; to seem to know the answers; wanting to win an argument rather than solve a problem; seeing one's ideas as truths to be defended.	6. Provisionalism: To be willing to experiment with your own behavior; to investigate issues rather than taking sides; to solve problems, not debate them.

From Gibb (1961).

1. Have I been judgmental in this process? Can I come up with a list of slurs to describe the person or the situation?

2. Have I been interested in punishing other people or in honestly solving the problem? (This relates to anger with the terminee. If feelings of betrayal, hostility, and anger exist it is difficult to have a problem-solving orientation.)

3. Have I been straightforward with people, letting them know openly where they have stood throughout their employment? (If the irritations have been held back, the answer is no.)

4. Can I understand how people can get into situations that would make them candidates for firing? Can I understand how it would feel to be pegged for a layoff?

5. Have I used positive terms to describe the employee? Is it easy for me to view the person without negative labels?

6. Do I have a need to prove to the other person and my peers that the position I have taken is right? Is termination what the other person needs in order to evaluate her/his career goals? Can I specify the factual reasons for this dismissal?

7. Can I accept the other person's explanation of situations and feelings, even though I may not agree? Am I ever willing to admit that I have made mistakes in the way I have worked with the employee?

8. Do I need to win every argument with the person, proving that he or she is wrong and rubbing it in?

The attitudes and messages that pass between managers and subordinates in the dismissal interview are volatile ones. Often the messages we send have an impact we never have intended. While we cannot control the event completely enough to avoid all tension in the interview, the awareness that certain attitudes foster more difficult interviews can be helpful.

Change

Many of us refer to ourselves as "creatures of habit." This can mean that we are people who need a certain amount of routine activity to keep us centered in our lives. When we experience drastic changes—whether or not we have initiated them—a certain amount of disorientation can be expected. Like divorces, terminations involve a greater-than-normal amount of disruption of normal everyday living. The disruption affects all parties concerned. A change expert, Ron Lippitt (1958), reminds us that change should be examined by considering the impact of the past, the present, and the future on the proposed change. Our fear of losing the past, disturbing the present, and facing the unknown future set the stage for this treatment of change.

Why even talk about change in this chapter? As managers, we are agents of change, even though we do not often think of ourselves that way. Any time we are involved in "changing the recurring pattern of behavior" (Kahn, 1974) in an organization, we are acting as agents of change. In this capacity, it can help us to understand how fear and change interact in our own perceptions to make the act of dismissing someone so difficult.

The Past: Looking Behind Us

In determining why terminations are so difficult to initiate, it is helpful to understand why inertia keeps dragging us away from the task. We often postpone action, hoping the situation will improve. To put it bluntly, we are reluctant to take the necessary initiative because of our investment in the past. Whether that past was good or bad, there is still a loyalty to it because it is our past, our history. If we hired the employee originally then we have a personal investment, a sense of responsibility. Merely because of its prior existence, it is difficult to unseat the impact the past has made upon us.

Consider how difficult it is to unseat the incumbent in a political race. Most elected officials have an invisible security that supports the re-election effort. Would-be replacements must come up with powerful arguments to overcome the loyalty to what has been. Likewise, inertia leads many people to stay in bad marriages. People remain in souring business partnerships or fail to renegotiate unfavorable contracts because of their solid commitment to past efforts.

A related issue is the question of our own identities. Who we are as managers is firmly rooted in our own past. People ask where we have been and what we have done. We respond by telling them the story of our lives. Take away this past and what becomes of us? Over a period of twelve years I taught in four colleges and universities. When I began to consult full-time, people would ask me what I did. I responded unconsciously, "I'm a college professor," even though technically that was not true. So strong was my investment in my own history that it was clear to others that I still viewed myself as an educator.

When we opt for a change, we bring our past into question. If we feel that our past actions will be viewed as if under a microscope, there is a tendency to take greater care. Self-examination is one thing, but inspection of our past encounters and handling of our business by others can be unsettling. The weight of the past to some extent also sanctions our present state of affairs.

Consider the case of John Warren, who worked for a Midwestern hospital for fifteen years without major incident. He had seen supervisors come and go, even though he himself was not a top-notch performer. He did just enough to avoid difficulty. Enter a new management team with higher performance expectations. Suddenly John's work was not good enough. His new supervisor had several talks with John about his performance, telling him that he wasn't "up there" with the rest of the employees. David Lister, the supervisor wanted to know why. "Well," John replied, "for fifteen years nobody complained. Why start now?" John's commitment was to the past. He could not assimilate the new demands and increased workload. He was not a part of the changed organization. Stubborn loyalty to "the way we were" creates friction for managers as well as for their employees.

As managers we can easily fall into the past trap. For example, Pat, a library administrator, had to deal with an employee and organizational history problem that she inherited from another supervisor. The employee came to her with glowing recommendations from her previous supervisor. The evaluations of the clerk's work encouraged Pat to view the clerk as a top-notch employee. However, little by little, Pat's impression changed and she began to doubt the truth of the recommendations. Jobs that were assigned to the clerk were routinely left half-done or undone. The employee was an avid reader who enjoyed the library environment. She could be found with her head stuck in a book during most of the workday. Her previous supervisor admired this attribute and evaluated her based on this devotion to reading. Pat, however, was more demanding and wanted to change the situation. Pat tried diplomatically to clarify the nature of the job expectations, but the employee disregarded her. She apparently felt that her recommendations were so good that no one would take any punitive actions. After three such conferences, Pat spoke with her supervisor about the problem. The supervisor could not believe what he heard. He had seen the recommendations and was astounded by Pat's counterevidence. It took Pat five more months to convince her superiors that the employee should be terminated. A major factor in the delay was the clerk's former boss, who continued to deny the truth of Pat's allegations.

It may be true that our pasts can come back to haunt us. Even when we have a desire to function in the present, focusing on the actual events and facts of any given situation, we should not assume that we are unaffected by what has gone before. The power the past exerts on our attitudes in dismissal are just as important as anything else. If we have had strained and uncomfortable feelings about prior terminations, it is easy to carry those old feelings into the new instance. Our goal must be to demonstrate to our own satisfaction that there is no reason why difficult times in the past must be duplicated. Otherwise our fears become a self-fulfilling prophecy.

To compensate for such sometimes unconscious behavior, clarify all the ways in which the current action differs from the previous action that presented trouble. Note how you have behaved differently and how the employee has behaved differently. Allow for the time that has passed between the two events. Surely we learn from experience—give yourself credit for that on-the-job training. What do you specifically want *not* to repeat? Given your 20/20 hindsight, what can you choose to do differently?

The Present: An Eye for the Moment at Hand

If, like most of the rest of the human race, you spend much of your free time considering the past or predicting the future, the present moment—a time we call *now*—is forgotten. This preoccupation with what we did ten minutes or ten years ago or what we will do ten minutes or ten years from now presents a dilemma for managers. With one leg in the past and one leg in the future, we are not in a position to make sound decisions in the now. Avoiding these twin temptations is not such an easy task. The past-future orientation helps ensure that our actions are grounded in fear.

To invoke termination proceedings against an employee demands that we give our undivided attention to the moment confronting us. Regardless of the frustration we may feel about the reasons for the dismissal, the decision to act brings about several disquieting results. First, the action alters the flow of events from past to present. It may jumble up what has seemed to be a nice, neat little package. The resulting disorder and confusion, which violates our business-as-usual mentality, is disturbing.

A second condition involves actually taking responsibility for making the decision. We act, confronting the present moment, overcoming the forces of inertia. In doing so we can be faced with many double binds. We know what happened in ancient times to messengers who brought bad news: they were killed. As bearers of bad news we may view ourselves as vulnerable messengers. A dismissal mandates a face-to-face meeting, a confrontation of the significant issues of the case, and mediation of the employee's reactions. All of these requirements may be difficult if we fear our ability to accomplish any one of them.

A third aspect of the present worthy of consideration is that dismissals interrupt the routine nature of our job. We are all involved in ordering, filling out reports, observing work progress, double-checking instructions, meeting with other department heads and colleagues. Terminations, however, are not an everyday experience. Because they tend to be more dramatic, we pay more attention to them. Firing is not something managers want to do often. Because terminations are generally spaced apart, it may seem that we have never initiated one before. We may actually forget what we did the last time.

The Future: The Desire to Predict

In our search for meaning in the termination process we can be confounded by the power of the past and by our discomfort with the present. A third force that looms on the horizon, the future, can make it equally difficult to manage the changing environment.

The future, which is not even here yet, makes some of us anxious. It is closely related to another skill some of us have developed into an art—worrying. We worry when we try to project into the future any insecurities we have about our current actions. Some typical worries related to termination interviewing include:

"What if the employee becomes uncontrollably angry?"

"What if the documentation won't hold up in court?"

"What if my boss thinks I botched the job?"

"What if they can't find a job?"

We might more productively ask ourselves why we are avoiding the issue. Worry wastes time and promotes paranoia. We can only deal with those what-if's to the extent that they do happen. No amount of time spent worrying is time well used. Those of us who are professional procrastinators probably have enough hours in worrying to have received a college degree in this timeless art. Since we have no crystal balls to foretell the future, we have only our efforts of the present to work with. Acting in good faith and following procedures are our best protection against the what-if syndrome.

A second way of looking at the bind the future can represent to us is connected to our own risk-taking behavior. If we see ourselves as low risk-takers we may have more trouble advancing termination actions. We may be convinced that the risk of instituting dismissal procedures far outweighs any possible advantages. The security of a sure thing is attractive to some people. We may keep our savings in the bank, avoiding higher-yield interest-bearing certificates. We are not willing to risk our assets for a better working environment.

The executive director of a transplant bank was distressed that her work team of highly trained individuals suffered because one person did not have a positive attitude, supporting the other members. The employee did not fit into the growth plan of the organization; she was holding the group back. In conferences with the employee it became clear that the attitude would not change. Since the person's dismissal, productivity has increased dramatically and the morale of the other professionals has changed for the better—all because the manager was willing to take the risk.

When we assume responsibility for the terminee's future and fail to terminate because of our fears for what will become of them, we have built a trap for ourselves that is hard to free ourselves from. Richard Irish's book, *If Things Don't Improve Soon I May Ask You to Fire Me* (1976), gives a fresh perspective to performance problems. The employee may be crying for help. The performance difficulty may be a vehicle for voicing dissatisfaction, boredom, or any number of other reactions. The employee may be indirectly maneuvering us to make a decision that he or she has avoided making.

At a recent professional conference, an executive in the television industry reported that he owed his career success to a magazine manager who ten years earlier had the good sense to fire him. He was bored with his job editing print material and his motivation to do a good job had all but evaporated. His boss simply talked about the drop in his desire to be there and asked him what he really wanted to be doing. He agreed that his heart was not in his job and that he needed to search for something involving audio as well as print production. Terminations can be a tool for personal development and a way of developing the organization.

Not all employees reach this point of reflection. It is hard for the employee who is laid off to recognize the positive value in the termination, especially if the person is in a trade that is experiencing structural unemployment. If there are no more jobs in a field, then retraining may be the only solution. The individual who cannot see himself or herself in another job or feels too old to learn something new may not benefit from the experience. However, in layoffs, it is the general good that must be paramount. There is some evidence that states and the federal government will sponsor retraining programs for displaced workers.

The Payoffs of Change

What can the payoffs be for the organization if a termination is appropriately made? It may mean that problems are solved and new opportunites arise. The change may reinforce company policies, it may allow the company to survive so it can support some employees rather than none, or it may mean that morale is improved. Of course there may be readjustment and acceptance time involved for those who remain, but these are natural processes. Because time lags for acceptance of the action are normal, they can be expected rather than feared.

We can help our organizations to consider termination as a more acceptable practice if we ask for careful development of guidelines and training in terminations. Many organizations manifest the same fear of terminations that individuals do. In examining the policies and procedures manuals of a number of organizations, the textbooks in personnel administration, we find little written about the actual termination. Historically organizations have wanted to presume that terminations were to be kept quiet. Morin and Yorks (1982) reviewed 1200 actual terminations and discovered (1) that actual termination interviews vary greatly from manager to manager with little corporate guidance, (2) that some managers try to soften the blow by hinting, with the result that the individual does not realize what is occurring, and (3) that others treat employees cruelly, attacking them personally as incompetent human beings. The wide range of behavior noticed by Morin and Yorks may result in large part from the lack of training in termination interviewing.

As we reevaluate the role of change in our decisions and actions of termination, the goal to strive for is the clear-thinking, concerned attitude that treats the event seriously, without erecting the barriers we introduce when we focus on the actions of the past or projections of the future.

SUMMARY

There are no panaceas that will magically transform all difficult situations into easy ones, nor would this be desirable. In dismissal interviews we are forced to confront our own foibles and human limitations. This chapter recognizes these truths and offers us a way of understanding dismissals that can help to explain their difficulty.

A working premise of the chapter is that fear is an integral part of our own felt difficulties with dismissal. It can permeate our understanding of our own conflict styles, the messages that we send to others, and the change process. Suggestions are made that give us a method for coping with fear by using Jampolsky's (1981) model of forgiveness.

The remainder of the chapter has explored the various arguments and reasons why our attitudes toward conflict may prevent us from responding reasonably to the event and the persons who are a part of it; why some of our encounters become more defensive than others; and why change creates problems for us as we consider terminating someone. Understanding each of these sources of difficulty can assist us in making sense of the dismissal, enabling us to plan for more effective separations with employees.

APPENDIX

I. YOU CAN'T FIRE ME!
II. I'M AFRAID I HAVE SOME BAD NEWS.
III. THAT'S NOT MY JOB!
IV. BUT I TRUSTED YOU, HOW COULD YOU DO THIS TO ME?
V. OH, COME ON! YOU REALLY DIDN'T MEAN IT.
VI. WAIT UNTIL I TELL EVERYONE WHAT AN OGRE YOU ARE!

Keep in mind that these vignettes are not necessarily exemplary interviews. Some cases may warrant termination—others may not. Some of the managers here have reacted out of frustration, impetuousness, caution, or empathy. All of these examples are excerpted from interviews conducted with managers experienced in the process of dismissal.

I. You Can't Fire Me!

Bob Birdwell, the newly transferred manager of a small hotel in New York City, had trouble on his hands. All of his department heads were ready to quit unless the chief engineer was fired. Andre, the engineer, had an authoritarian streak. He constantly argued with other department heads and could not accept honest criticism. In general he was a thorn in everyone's side. Technically he was a good engineer. Bob knew that Andre could destroy his operation with the flip of a switch because of his knowledge of the physical plant. How to proceed?

Fully prepared to deal with Andre's unruly temper, Bob called in a witness—a huge security guard. He feared Andre's volatile temperament. Dreading the firing, Bob had postponed it. As he had predicted, the engineer was enraged. He began to curse, getting red in the face. He yelled, "You can't do this to me!" Bob let him get it all off his chest, then began to talk about the sizable severance package. Bob fully expected retaliation. Andre left immediately. There was no retaliation.

II. I'm Afraid I Have Some Bad News.

In a last-ditch effort to remain solvent, a grocery chain modernized its stores and opened a state-of-the-art prototype store in a rapidly growing community. The innovative store soon became a hub of socializing. It offered items that had never been available in the town before. Workers from the chain's older store asked to be transferred to the new facility. The future looked bright. The profitability of this store, however, could not offset the losses incurred by the chain as a whole. No more than two months after its grand opening, corporate headquarters notified all stores that a general shutdown would occur within a month.

Kay, a longtime employee, had trained all the cashiers for the new store. As the supervisor of all the cashiers she had jumped at the opportunity to train in a larger facility. She had hoped the store would be purchased by another large chain. Ironically, the old store where she had worked for ten years was bought, but not the new store. Kay's manager, Jim, was leaving also. Jim had to tell Kay her job was eliminated. He began by saying, "I'm afraid I have some bad news, Kay." Kay noticed Jim had a hard time looking her in the eyes, perhaps trying to shield her from seeing that his eyes were brimming with tears. "As you know," he said, "we have not found a buyer for this store. Our old store has been purchased, but the new owner will not allow us to transfer employees to that store. This is just rotten luck for all of us. You know as well as I do this says nothing about how well we have done our jobs. Tell me what you'll do."

"Well, Jim," Kay stuttered, "I have two kids in junior high school and my husband's job at the plant looks okay. I want to work. I guess I hadn't really believed they would let me go. Never thought I would be pounding the streets looking for another job. I was real satisfied. I guess what I need to know now are things about references, the profit-sharing plan, those kind of things. I'm pretty lucky—at least there's another income for us. Some of the guys in produce have wives that don't work."

Jim sighed, "I wish there was something to do. It's just such a damned shame. This store was doing so well. But, there isn't much left except to close the place."

III. That's Not My Job!

The case of Mary Marks's termination of Willie Brown, a hospital janitor, is not as straightforward as Jim's store closing. One incident convinced Mary that Willie had to leave the hospital. On Willie's shift a nurse had overturned a cafeteria cart. In her embarrassment and attempt to right things she called Willie to the scene and demanded that he clean up the mess immediately. Willie shook his head, saying, "I'm only supposed to sweep up around here." The nurse, amazed at his denial, called the supervisor over to order Willie to clean up the mess.

With the second request, Willie met it with the same reply. "I'm only supposed to sweep up around here." When he refused a second time, the nursing supervisor marched him down to the sanitation manager for action. Willie complained and admonished the supervisor, "You shouldn't be doing this." Willie was infuriated and upset by this unnecessary trouble. He muttered under his breath about the parentage of the nursing supervisor.

In the manager's office, Willie continued to verbally attack the nursing supervisor. The manager described him as emotionally confused in the interview. Willie began citing examples of other employees who had done worse than he. He was told that other employees had nothing to do with his difficulty. In an attempt to end the encounter, the manager told Willie not to report back for work, saying that his final check would be available in two hours in the personnel office.

The maintenance manager said she hated to see people act this way and so terminated Willie to solve a problem. This situation is a classical example of an incident snowballing into a dismissal. Willie did not challenge his discharge for disobeying orders.

IV. But I Trusted You, How Could You Do This to Me?

Mary, the manager of a large metropolitan grocery store, had worked with Mrs. Lee for four years. Mrs. Lee had been in this country for ten years. Mary had trusted Mrs. Lee to open the store for her upon occasion. It came as a shock to Mary that security suspected Mrs. Lee of stealing money from the company in the way she rang up items on the cash register. Security sent a spot shopper into her line and videotaped the transaction. The evidence was clear that Mrs. Lee was taking money from the register. Mary felt awful—she liked the woman! Company policy dictated that security remove her from the store and notify her of automatic suspension. When Mary did talk with Mrs. Lee several days later, the woman had aged. Humiliated and contrite, Mrs. Lee promised to pay back every cent she had taken. She made restitution in lieu of the filing of formal charges against her.

V. Oh, Come On! You Really Didn't Mean It.

Jerry Rice, a cable television executive, had a dismaying experience with a divisional sales manager, Don, who refused to accept that he had been fired. Jerry felt that firing Don in the office was in poor taste, so he took the sales manager to a bar for a drink, thinking this was more civilized. He told Don he was being terminated because he had not turned in his expense reports for the last year.

This was not a new issue between them. Don had been with the firm for three years and thought he was going to the top. The man was a real wheeler dealer. At the restaurant he took the message "like a man," admitting that he was a little surprised. He said he understood everything.

As Don's termination began to sink in, Jerry received fourteen phone calls from him, begging Jerry to let him come back. Fourteen times Jerry explained that Don could not come back. When Jerry became angry during the last call, the former sales manager stopped calling.

VI. Wait Until I Tell Everyone What An Ogre You Are!

Whether it is an employee who has a hard time accepting the decision or one who becomes belligerent, the impact on the manager may be telling. Bob Hawkins, manager of a popular steak restaurant, had established an incentive program for his workers. The employees could earn complimentary dinners for friends if their attendance records were exemplary. One of his prize waiters was abusing the system. Thinking that a warning would suffice, Bob mentioned that the system was a generous one, but that inviting several friends over a short period of time was an abuse.

It happened again. Bob called the waiter into his office with the assistant manager. He sat the waiter down, saying, "You are a good waiter, one of the best. However, rules are rules. I warned you about abusing the complimentary dinner program. It was to stop." The waiter cried and begged to work until Saturday. Bob agreed.

Saturday night at a birthday party the waiter told all the other employees that Bob had nailed him for a minor violation and he couldn't be trusted. Needless to say, Bob faced a hostile audience when Sunday evening serving started. He called in one of the most popular waiters in to discuss the overt hostility. Realizing they were upset about the termination, he explained the cause and clarified the complimentary incentive program. Before the week was out the antagonism was gone and work was back to normal.

If any of these vignettes bring back memories for us of events we handled well or poorly, they have served their purpose. The ultimate test for many of us may be to ask ourselves whether we would want to be dismissed the way we have dismissed employees. Putting ourselves in the shoes of others can provide important cues about our own capacities.

REFERENCES

Albert, S., and Kessler, S. 1976. Processes for ending social encounters: Conceptual archaeology of a temporal place. *Theory of Social Behavior,* 6: 2, 147–170.

Alsop. R. 1980. Some basic rules for managers to follow when an employee has to be dismissed. *Wall Street Journal,* 103 (81): 29.

Altman, I., and Taylor, D. A. 1973. *Social penetration: the development of interpersonal relationships.* New York: Holt, Rinehart, and Winston.

Appraising the performance appraisal. 1980. *Business Week,* 2637 (May 19): 153–154.

Avins, A. *Penalties for Misconduct on the Job.* 1972. Dobbs Ferry, NY: Oceana Publications.

Ball, R. R. 1978. What's the answer to performance appraisal? *The Personnel Administrator,* 23 (July): 43–46.

Baytos, L. 1979. Easing the pain of terminations. *Personnel,* 56: 64–69.

Blake, R., and Mouton, J. S. 1979. O.D.: Fad or fundamental? *Training and Development,* 33 (1): 110–117.

Brinkerhoff, D. W., and Kanter, R. M. 1980. Appraising the performance of performance appraisal. *Sloan Management Review,* 22 (Spring): 3–14.

Burger, C. 1972. *Creative firing.* New York: Collier Books.

Burger, C. 1972. The ritual of firing executives. *International Management,* 9: 45–48.

Buzzotta, V. R., and Lefton, R. E. 1978. How healthy is your performance appraisal system? *The Personnel Administrator,* 23 (August): 48–51.

Clutterbuck, D. 1976. Helping managers improve performance appraisal. *International Management,* 31 (November): 41–46.

Conner, R. D., and Fjerstad, R. L. 1974. Internal personnel maintenance. In D. Yonder and H. G. Heneman, eds., *Staffing policies and strategies,* 4-234–4-235. Washington, DC: American Society for Personnel Administration and Industrial Relations/Bureau of National Affairs.

Cook, D. 1981. Whistleblowers: friend or foe? *Industry Week,* 211: 51–56.

Coulson, R. 1981. *The termination handbook.* New York: Free Press.

Deal, T., and Kennedy, A. 1982. *Corporate cultures: the rites and rituals of corporate life.* Reading, MA: Addison-Wesley.

Downs, C. W., Smeyak, G. P. and Martin, E. 1980. *Professional interviewing.* New York: Harper and Row.

Feeney, A. 1981. When life in the executive suite turns sour. *Colorado Business,* 2: 39–41.

Fiedler, F., Chemers, M., and Mahar, L. 1977. *Improving leadership effectiveness.* New York: John Wiley and Sons.

Filley, A. 1975. *Interpersonal conflict resolution.* Glenview, IL: Scott Foresman.

Finley, M., and Lee, T. 1981. The terminated executive: it's like dying. *The Personnel and Guidance Journal,* 59 (6): 382–383.

Firing the incompatible employee. 1962. *Supervision,* 24 (7): 15.

Flanagan, J. C. 1954. The critical incident technique. *Psychological Bulletin,* 51 (4): 327–357.

Following established procedures. 1962. *Supervision,* 24 (7): 15.

Frost, J., and Wilmot, W. 1978. *Interpersonal conflict.* Dubuque, IA: Wm. C. Brown.

Garrison, L., and Ferguson, J. 1977. Separation interview. *Personnel Journal,* 56 (9): 438–442.

Gibb, J. 1961. Defensive communication. *The Journal of Communication,* 11 (3): 141–148.

Hakel. M. D., and Dunnette, M. 1970. *Checklists for describing job applicants.* Minneapolis: Industrial Relations Center.

Heizer, J. H. 1976. Transfer and terminations as staffing options. *Academy of Management Journal,* 19 (1): 115–120.

Hinrichs, J. 1980. Aspiring to fall. *Psychology Today,* 17 (10): 25–26.

Hudgens, A. G. 1983. A whistleblower's daily treasure. Dallas: E.P.I.C. Publications.

Hugo, J. L. 1982. The relative value of communication skills in the appraisal of employee performance. M.S. thesis, University of Denver.

Irish, R. 1976. *If things don't improve soon I may ask you to fire me: the management book for everyone who works.* Garden City, NJ: Anchor Press.

Jampolsky, G. 1981. Love is letting go of fear. New York: Bantam Books.

Jandt, F. 1973. *Conflict resolution through communication.* New York: Harper and Row.

Kaagen, S. 1978. Terminating people from key positions. *Personnel Journal,* 57 (2): 96–98.

Kahn, R. 1974. Organizational development: some problems and proposals. *Journal of Applied Behavioral Sciences,* 10: 4.

King, P. 1984. How to prepare for a performance appraisal interview. *The Training and Development Journal*, 38 (2): 66–69.

King, P. 1984. *Performance planning and appraisal*. New York: McGraw-Hill Book Co.

Knapp, M. 1978. *Social intercourse: from greeting to good-bye*. Boston: Allyn and Bacon.

Knapp, M., Hart, R., and Freidrich, G. 1973. The rhetoric of good-bye: verbal and nonverbal correlates of human leave-taking. *Speech Monographs*, 40:182–198.

Koch, S., and Deetz, S. 1981. Metaphor analysis of social reality in organizations. *Journal of Applied Communication Research*, 9 (1): 1–15.

Kravetz, D. 1978. Counseling strategies for involuntary terminations. *Personnel Administrator*, 23 (10): 438–442.

Lippitt, G. 1969. *Organizational Renewal*. New York: Appleton-Century Crofts.

Lippitt, R., Watson, J., and Westley, B. 1958. *The dynamics of planned change*. New York: Harcourt Brace and World.

Mayeske, G. W., Harman, F. L., and Glickman, A. S. 1966. What can critical incidents tell management? *Training and Development Journal*, 20 (4): 20.

Meyer, H., Kay, E., and French, J., Jr. 1965. Split roles in performance appraisal. *Harvard Business Review*, 43: 123–129.

Michal-Johnson, P. 1981. Defensive and relational communication correlates of the termination interview. Ph.D. thesis, University of Denver.

Mirvis, P., and Lawler, E., III. 1977. Measuring the financial impact of employee attitudes. *Journal of Applied Psychology*, 62: 1–18.

Mobley, W. 1982. *Employee turnover: causes, consequences and control*. Menlo Park, CA: Addison-Wesley.

Morin, W., and Cabrera, J. 1982. *Parting company: how to survive the loss of a job and find another successfully*. New York: Harcourt, Brace and Jovanovich.

Morin, W., and Yorks, L. 1982. *Outplacement techniques: a positive approach to terminating employees*. New York: Harcourt, Brace and Jovanovich.

On the firing line: a gentler approach. 1967. *Sales Management*, 98 (3): 56–57.

O'Reilly, C, and Weitz, B. 1980. Managing marginal employees: the use of warnings and dismissals. *Administrative Science Quarterly*, 25 (3): 467–484.

Personal business. 1971. *Business Week*, 2189: 91.

Peters, T. J., and Waterman, R. H., Jr. 1984. *In search of excellence: lessons from America's best-run companies*. New York: Warner Books.

Pre-discharge checklist. 1963. *Supervision*, 25 (4): 21.

Resnick, S., and Mohrman, A., Jr. 1982. The design of performance appraisal systems: some implications from research findings. *International Association for Personnel Women Journal*, Fall: 7–10.

Rosenfeld, L. 1976. *Now that we're all here*. Columbus, Ohio: Charles E. Merrill, 61–62.

Sauser, W. I., Jr. 1980. Evaluating employee performance: needs, problems, and possible solutions. *Public Personnel Management,* 9 (Jan.-Feb.): 11–17.

Schmidt, W. 1984. The exit interview as monitor of change: a review of the literature. Presented at the Southern Speech Communication Association conference, Baton Rouge, LA.

Schmitt, N. 1976. Social and situational determinants of interview decisions: implications for the employment interview. *Personnel Psychology,* 29: 79–101.

Schreier, J. 1980a. Training for terminations. *Training and Development Journal,* 12: 50–53.

Schreier, J. 1980b. Terminations: putting the pieces together. Unpublished manuscript, Milwaukee, WI: Marquette University.

Sieburg, E. 1976. Confirming and disconfirming organizational communication. In J. Owens, P. Pager, and G. Zimmerman (eds.), *Communication in organizations.* New York: West Publishing Co. 129–149.

Sincoff, M., and Goyer, R. 1984. *Interviewing.* New York: Macmillan.

Smith, P. 1984. Performance Planning and Appraisal.

Steinmetz, L. 1968. What to do about poor performers. *Supervisory Management* 13 (7): 2–7.

Stewart, C., and Cash, W. 1982. *Interviewing: principles and practices.* Dubuque, IA: William C. Brown, 236–239.

Stybel, L. 1978. *Managing human resource termination: the interpersonal conduct and organizational consequences of executive dismissal.* Ph.D. thesis, Harvard University, Cambridge, MA.

Sweet, D. 1975. *Decruitment.* Reading, MA: Addison-Wesley.

Sweet, D. 1979. What's wrong with being fired? *Personnel Journal,* 692.

Tarrant, J. J. 1974. *Getting fired: an American ordeal.* Cincinnati: Van Nostrand Reinhold.

The dwindling right to fire. 1960. *Fortune,* 62 (2): 204.

To fire or not to fire. 1958. *Supervisory Management,* 3 (1): 22–25.

Wallace, M. J., Crandall, N. F., and Fay, C. 1982. *Administering human resources: an introduction to the profession.* New York: Random House.

Wells, T. 1980. *Keeping your cool under fire: communicating nondefensively.* San Francisco: McGraw-Hill Book Co.

Westcott, R. F. 1976. How to fire an executive. *Business Horizons,* 19 (2): 33–36.

When dismissal is the answer. 1963. *Supervisory Management,* 8 (3): 48–50.

When you fire an employee. 1967. *Administrative Management,* 28 (4): 12.

Woodman, L. 1973. *Perspectives in self-awareness; essays on human problems.* Columbus: Charles E. Merrill.

Zemke, R. 1979. The critical incident method of analysis. *Training/HRD,* April: 67–68.

INDEX